Adventures in Ancient Egypt

ADVENTURES
IN ANCIENT EGYPT

P O E M S

Albert Goldbarth

OHIO STATE UNIVERSITY PRESS
Columbus

Goldbarth, Albert.
    Adventures in Ancient Egypt : poems / Albert Goldbarth.
       p.   cm.
    ISBN 0-8142-0714-6 (cloth : alk. paper). — ISBN 0-8142-0715-4
    (paper)
       I. Title.
    PS3557.O354A65   1996
    811'.54—dc20   96-29472
                                                                 CIP

Text and cover design by Donna Hartwick.
Cover illustration: *Pyramids* miniature painting by Fanny Brennan.
Type set in Garamond by Brevis Press, Bethany, Connecticut.
Printed by Braun-Brumfield, Inc., Ann Arbor, Michigan.

9   8   7   6   5   4   3   2   1

acknowledgments

Poems in this collection originally appeared in the following journals:

Agni: "The Saga of Stupidity and Wonder"

The Bellingham Review: "Real Speeches"

The Berkeley Review: "Own Recognizable"

The Black Warrior Review: "The Route," "What the Poem Is Actually About"

Boulevard: "Ancient Semitic Rituals for the Dead"

The Cimarron Review: "Deer"

The Cream City Review: "Repairwork"

The Gettysburg Review: "The Compasses"

The Laurel Review: "Ancient Stories (Stop Me If You've Heard This One Before)"

The North Dakota Quarterly: "The Lives of the—Wha'?"

The Ontario Review: "Meop"

Poetry: "Circa 1861," "Poem Beginning with a Quote from Keith Laumer's *Galactic Odyssey* and Ending with a Quote from Mika Waltari's *The Egyptian*," "Prepositions"

Poetry East: "In the x-ray of the sarcophagus of Ta-pero"

The Southwest Review: "A Still Life, Symbolic of Lines"

Western Humanities Review: "This Needle's Tip,"

▲

"The Compasses" was also reprinted in *Harper's.*

"A Still Life, Symbolic of Lines" was also reprinted in *The Best American Poetry 1995.*

▲

The sequence "Ancient Musics" was originally published as a limited edition chapbook in the *feuillets* series from Helicon Nine Editions.

"Because of their fossils" was originally published in the chapbook *Ten Poets* (The Wing and the Wheel Press).

▲

Note: "Qebehseneuf" was originally published in *The Ontario Review* and reprinted in *Popular Culture* (Ohio State University Press, 1990). Its subject is, in part, my mother's then forthcoming (and, at the time of writing, unforeseeably successful) operation for colon cancer. It takes its now proper place in the sequence "Ancient Egypt/Fannie Goldbarth" in the current book. The following poem, "Repairwork," is from that same period of time. The four poems ending the sequence, however, are more recent in origin.

Likewise, "Sumerian Votive Figurines" was originally published in *The Ontario Review* and subsequently in *The Gods* (Ohio State University Press, 1993). It is reincluded here, as the appropriate introduction to the sequence of prose poems that constitute the main body of the section "Ancient Musics."

▲

Special thanks to David Baker, David Citino, Mark Cox, Christopher Howell, and Gloria Vando, for encouragement at various way stations; and to Mark Polizzotti, for the freedom.

For some considerable time there has been a lack of a general synthesis of ancient Egyptian funerary practices in a form which would be suitable both for the general reader and for students of Egyptology. . . . It was with these problems in mind that this book was initiated.

A. J. SPENCER, *Death in Ancient Egypt*

▲

contents

INTRODUCTION

In the x-ray of the sarcophagus of Ta-pero

of the Twenty-second Dynasty, we see the skull
is fit inside its gilded wooden covering-face
as perfectly as thought is, in a sleeping brain,
or music is, in a radio that's *off*
—it's waiting to flower from this
body-of-the-moment. You ask me:
what do *I* know of ancient Egypt?—

almost nothing. A couple of coffee-table books.
A couple of lecture series with slides.
And that at night sometimes, in the zero of night,
I've felt the weight of another head
inside of my head, leaning its skull
against my skull as if to rest—it's traveled such a long,
long way and still has so far to go.

ANCIENT STORIES

Stop Me If You've Heard
This One Before

She's scratching her name on a weathered block of rose-granite.
Because her name is (commonly) Ann, it's been written innumerable
times before in history; and if I wanted to think of *pre*history,
everything has happened before, exact or approximate: somewhere
in between those poles, for instance, ontogeny makes of any
one of us the latest repetition of a multibrachiate Darwintree
of ancestry—of feather-us, and gill-us, and ciliawriggle-us—
in a tunnel of time that goes from a woman birth-contracting (here,
now) on the bed of a trash Ford pickup, back
to a water before there was any dry land at all. Whew.
Also: *Hadnakhte,* "scribe of the treasury," proudfully left his name
and time graffito'd on the wall of a chapel of Djoser's pyramid,
1244 B.C.—the need would seem to be built into us,
to say "I'm here." She carves *Ann* with a diamond

▲

from the cluster on her wedding ring and then,
with a crazy insousiance, slings the band over her shoulder
into the desert sands (much guide-boy scrimmage here).
The truth is: this is the story of a typically been-around,
dour-puss woman, someone whose incessant bicker
kept the life of a husband substantially smaller than it
otherwise might have been—as if she gnawed away
at the edges of possibilities. And this is a story
about the man, who every night tumbled home with the little
wage of a day at the dyeworks pissed away
in a mossy trough out back of Mack-O's Hi Tyme Bar,
a story of fists, a story of seven years of fists and a belt
he'd whirr around with the buckle-end
connecting. She left. She packed their baby Annie

▲

in a wicker picnic hamper and left, ~~some said~~
~~to an aunt and a laundress job in Schenectady but~~
some said to a Cuban drug king lover with almondine skin
and a seventeen-room Miami mansion. No one
knows; in any case that story is over. If any story is over,
ever. Lucretius (circa 60 B.C.): *solidity*
is compounded of its irreducible units,
which he calls *atoms,* and *these*
lie far below the range of our ungenerous sight
and *exist in all things, in admixture with vacuity*
—knowledge lost for two millennia, then rediscovered
in terms of Newton, Heisenberg, Bohr. A woman
leaves a husband; twenty-one years after that,
her daughter leaves a husband—leaves, in fact,

▲

her whole bemired life, for two escapist weeks
of touring: leaving the pyramid now, aware of the guide-boys staring
aware of her lean American beauty: a flower
smolders in her black hair like a torch on an ebony wall.
So—are we destined to living out predetermined patterns?
Are we shackled? The undergraduate
philosophy major thinks so, walks his city at midnight
fuming—past Tee's Discount Hardware Store,
the Temple of Unified Light, the Pinball Palace—fuming,
in his twenty-year-old's sense of intergalactic injustice,
fuming: but believing it: we're born to reenact
what we're born *of*. You can't read history or sociology
wide-awake and *not* see that. The beaten
beat someone. The rich get richer. Even

▲

so reductive and arguable, the idea of limiting
humankind by fate, by preordainment, has him
(beerily powered) shaking his fist in rant at the stars
—but then, remember, he's twenty, and a student,
in a student's life: he has no wife to rant at
(really no confining dailiness of any kind but classes)
and, like anyone, he needs to rail at *something*. And
as for those baleful stars . . .   they're being praised
an hundredfold as a billowy incense rises,
and a lyrically doctrinal passage rises as well,
at the Temple of Unified Light: a midnight service
savvily copied after someone's researched
notion of Ancient Mystery Rites: a priestess singing
mesmerizing gush about the soul,

▲

in its cyclical visits, trying on and doffing
human bodies like gowns in a hock shop—maybe
phoneybaloney to some; to others, a transporting
metaphysical belief that makes confusion and ambivalence
the small parts of a larger, processional order. Makes
this short song we call "being alive," and its silence, "death,"
the melody-line of a composition endlessly working poignant
variation and refrain. "In a previous life,
in Atlantis, I was the chiefmost sanctum consort of the God.
I never fed myself. They bathed me in an onyx basin
of asses' milk." "In Babylon . . . / In slave days
maybe in Alabama or Georgia before the War . . . /
In ancient Egypt I awaited my love in the marshes,
for my love is a tall proud reed." But

▲

we don't need to tithe at the Temple of Unified Light
to find our own camcorderheadlinegossipdramafests
prefigured in the glory and horror of, say,
dynastic Egypt. I put my ear to the 10 o'clock news
and hear, from its pith, its magma: "We have smote
the infidels' cult-place, we have made of them charred ruin,
their soldiers' bodies we have stacked head-high." It
isn't just war: the locus-and-deployment of
fatiguing strength along the arms of this figurine of a woman
rolling dough (about 2200 B.C.) is that of the laundress
Degas tenderly renders in pastels. I put my ear
to the Top Ten station: "I awaited my love
in the marshes, for my love is a tall proud reed.
In the wind of my longing he shudders." Or listen:

▲

I waited over an hour after the hockey game—the asswipe.
Pam was gone for the week, she gave me a key to that room
she had in those days, over the pissy stink of Mack-O's.
It did fine, though. I was wanting it so *bad—I never told*
no one this, so hush—that when he finally rapped on the door
I came. We stayed in that room for three days straight.
It was winter . . . / The snow was lush, romantic
doilies floating down as slowly as if through water.
Then it's mid-October. On the bed
of a trash Ford pickup, seven miles from the hospital
and seven days before he's shipped to 'Nam, she
Jesus Jesus Jesus spasms Ann Elizabeth
into the jouncing (bad shocks) world. It's one more
variant of The Only Story There Is, and it begins

▲

with the explosive birth of Totality from the Original Dot
—the Original Spacetime Dot of Coterminous Everything—
some 15 billion years ago. The universe is
the daily iteration of this, from photons, from mitosis,
to the clumsily connective workings-out of human desire.
Speaking of which . . .   the Cairo Plaza Hotel by night
is rich in sexual promise. Camel-kick liqueurs.
Dark corners. She knows in a week she'll be back in the States,
enrolled in Computer Programming 1 at the U. Ho hum.
Tonight, though . . .   men wink sheikh-eyes at her, men
in thousand-dollar suits, they trail her like ellipses, and
she's tipsy with this power. Why does it feel we've
heard this story before? The golden oldies fill our heads,
our hearts are thick with reruns. "The other woman's story

▲

became hers," Richard Russo says in his novel *Mohawk*.
Yes, and in a similar way, the story that starts
at the ten-to-the-minus-forty-third-of-a-second
of the Ur-Explosion, before there was matter,
before there were *waves* or *particles* of matter—a story not so much of birth
and death, but a story of ultimate states and their continuous
recombination—is everybody's biography. A woman
is muttering: "Ingrate. The bitch, the ingrate. Never
calls me, visits, nothing. *Pfui*—" she spits out the window
"—such a way to treat a mother." This she says to the sky
~~above the laundry~~ above her drug lord's Florida mansion
as if the sky has never heard of such maltreatment before.
The sun sets off Miami's coast. ~~The sun sets over Schenectady.~~
There's nothing new under it, Shakespeare says. In Cairo

▲

16

tonight, so far in degree from the hotel lights, it
may as well be centuries instead of city blocks,
a split-lipped guide-boy with a diamond in his hip-purse
stands his pals to a rowdy, blowsy good time; and, ooh
that American (*sway-sway*-motion-with-both-hands) woman!
Their bold, appreciative laughter. I've heard that laughter:
I've been to Mack-O's Hi Tyme Bar. I've gladly
shucked myself of the soiled skin of one more day,
there, in its easy banter and hard-luck looks,
I've swallowed its suds and its guy jokes. Somewhere else,
the women are talking: *How is a man like linoleum?*
Lay him right the first time, and you can walk
all over him. Laughter that the dark has heard
drift over the world's first cooking fires. And Ann?—

▲

will one day dawdle after classes at the Pinball Palace,
there to meet our philosophy major, sweet manboy
. . . but that's another story. For now, she's sleepily leaning
over a hotel balcony, greeting the upbursting sun
like some twentieth-century muezzin. When we met her,
she was proclaiming "I'm here"—as if declaring
a temporal singularity, in the history of *I'm here*s
on the sills of Pompeii, on the painted plinths of the Confederacy,
on the beerhouse walls of Atlantis . . .   I'm going to
sign this poem. I'm going to leave a line for you:

_____.

I'm here is the submost unit of the universe.
She plucks the draggled flower from her hair, and tosses it willynilly
into the wind that scours the stones of ancient and modern Egypt.

ANCIENT MUSICS

Sumerian Votive Figurines

were meant to pray, unceasingly, on their owners' behalfs.
He thinks: they still might, even though the proper recipient
gods have long since gone to theology mulch; this faith is
stone and for the most part unbroken. Choired-up
this way—there's an even dozen he's studying—something
hushed and intercessionary *does* texture the air in a circle
around their geometricized devotional posture. Some were done
300 years apart, and yet a gentle uniformity attends these
stand-in men and women; he thinks of his own
world's fashions of 300 years ago, then shakes his head, because
what kind of halfass world-class Sumerologist *is* he, dizzy
at the edge of cracked conjecture when he should be adding up facts?
In any case, it's lunchtime: baloney-and-curry on white with
chocolate cream-filled Ooh-Oohs for dessert, and the mail is letters
from both of his kids. He shakes his head again, he needs to: Lou, poor
Lou, was nabbed two years ago by the FBI for harboring a stolen
circus elephant (the poop of which contained ten bags
of paradise-quality coke, though Lou persuasively argued ignorance), then
Becky (spouses always sensing the moment of thinnest defense
in one another) left on the day of his trial, left with someone
who styled himself (or so the script across the leather jacket blared)
The King of Venusian Blues, whatever that was (or wherever). Melanie,
meanwhile, couldn't be more jet-propelled successful; every week,
it seems, her company ("The Company," she says, like "Truth" or "Eternity")
eats some smaller companyette, and while she once was Lord Almighty
of its Alabama xerox network, now she oversees
the "coastal-corridor/Europe conglomerate" for an empire of
"communications outreach" where, so far as he can tell from what
she patiently details, you can press a button in DC and, *whoosh*,
two blueprints, a bundle of money the size of a basketball, and, if
you want, a troupe of lubriciously spangled naiads tumbles
from a cloud of hi-tech pixie dust into a boardroom in Rome.
There are photos, from each, of the grandkids: Sonny
sporting a t-shirt tricked up with an airbrushed skull on fire
vomiting various barnyard animals; and Darlene

21

in a ballerina's tutu making her porky four-year-old's body
look, he'd swear, as if it just passed a very diaphanous fart.
It could make a man—what? guffaw? weep? or
see it's 5 p.m. by now and shake his head, and grab his lunchbox
(painted by Estelle to be an Assyrian sphinx) and head home.
Each day, five days a week, for seven years, he's exited this freeway
at BUBBA'S LAWN ORNAMENTS PAINTED OR PLAIN, and
nodded at the plaster hundreds grouped below its awning: gnomes
(whose bases reveal they're Lumpy, Dumpy, and Frumpy), fawns
and bucks, a contingent of Venus de Milos and several representatives
from the world of bare-shouldered flamenco danseuses,
bulbous-bottomed hausfraus with their bloomers comically skewed,
globe-helmeted deep-sea divers with overspilling treasure chests,
a number of Iwo Jima flag-raisings, artichoke-derriered mermaids
and their trident-bearing paramours, guardian lions, borzois
(he *thinks* they're borzois: *some* kind of italicized dog), assorted
Viking warriors and strikingly-bonneted Indian chiefs
with feathered spears, and seemingly endless frogs and mice and turtles
wearing human attire—snoods or zoot-suits or biker garb. . . .
Okay then, pray for *my* people, he tells them.

Ancient Egyptian Canopic Jars

(she's learned now, as she sauntered with a light tick-tock of her spandexed hips down the dim Archeology corridors of the museum) were the vessels, stone or clay or wood, in which the fished-out organs of the dead would be stored, so brought like matching luggage toward Eternity alongside their eviscerated body. Okay; but why does she *keep on thinking* of them, even once she reluctantly steps from the museum (she was spending a solo lunchbreak there) and, on the way back to the Fitness Center, mingles inside this ragtag range of noontime lingerers watching a street musician set up?

This leftover hipster with bird-doo'd beret and slipping, clicking, splayed polymer teeth; this tangerine-dungareed woman with earrings the size of locker padlocks and LESBIAN OLD-TIME FIDDLERS ALLIANCE button niftily gleaming; this guy she's seen before with the . . . ferret? or mongoose? . . . an *ottery* thing, whatever, on a clothesline leash. . . .

As if she's goggled in "x-ray spex" from out of a comic book's backpage ads, she sees them as baklava-like layer-in-layer of tissuey *dermis,* with the living coiled sluice and fisting meat of their deepest linkages on display. —The "marrow fruits," her grandmother called those bloody bundles, or sometimes "swampgut roses"— chucking the tripe-pile out of a capon's rubbery purple-lipped rend.

The liver (Imset), the stomach (Duwamutef), the bowel (Qebehseneuf), the lungs (Hapy), each in its cylindrical container, each in the care of its individual sentinel-deity. What a neatly fourplex schema to make of our otherwise unmanageable interior! They even partitioned what we call "the soul," as Newton did white light: the *ka,* the *ba,* the *sahu,* and the *khu:* a world where spirit was composite, like a chord, or color wheel, and could be diagrammed!

Of course, she thinks, that makes sense in a universe whose basic rule is division of all of existence into the mighty and the not (you know: the high Nabobs, and the low Joes). Or maybe it sometimes *did* get interestingly blurrier in its distinctions: one of the placards said a mouse and a lizard were accidentally wrapped in with a mummy, one was found that held the leg bones of a bird, and often one "whole" mummy was actually chicanerously splatched together from several dismembered corpses, grab-bag toe-bones and pottery bitlets bridging any unevenness. And *then* what?—waking resurrected and shielding your eyes from the Glory with what you suddenly realize is not your arm but an ibis wing? This backroom crack-and-grafting is the Afterlife's genetic engineering, on the scale of platters of chicken ribs.

It's gods with the heads of crocodiles, it's women and men in the halls of Forever with cat femurs rattling inside them. It's all so lollapalooza circusy, it's . . . well, it's something like shuffling about this growing midtown crowd, this fractured expressionist welter of democracy, and she knows she'll never make it back to Jazzercise 1 on time, no, now she's loitering, connoitering, she's here amid muumuu, tutu, dashiki, tarboosh, babushka, wimple, shako, and sequinned tube-top, here where a man fine-tuning an invisible rocketship console in front of him nudges a woman as still as a marble icon, who models what seems a single perfectly-gouged piranha-bite out of her forearm. Here, the dour, dough-jowled dowager's crowding the sleek *artiste* with hair dyed to look like an endive, who's holding a canvas that seems as if pinworms dipped in paint held orgiastic congress across it. And skins: the mineral-color of curry, the color of butter streusel, of oxblood polish! The freckles! The frizzled hair in the ears!

And now somebody festooned with a necklace as lush as a lei (but the "flowers" are fashioned of trashcan scraps, used foil, coathanger wire, madras-pattern wrapping tissue); and now the little boy crouched down like a picnic hamper; and now the little girl jitterbugging her sugar-rush out of her system; and now Osiris appearing amidst the crowd as the street musician carefully pours apportioned water into his homemade "hydrophone," and Horus the Hawk, and Isis, and Nut, whose plexus-wrenchingly beautiful naked body is the sky itself that shelters-over the world and over this street in the world where our own dear bodies no matter how frail are gathered, are stuffed with love and tumors and tremulous nodes, and the music begins, and each jar holds its own one whole clear note.

The Ark of the Covenant

out of glazed polymer resins: "your choice of corals or blues" . . . The Ark of the Covenant out of sculpted whitefish, "with horseradish trim" . . .

She knows that from the pages of this inventively tacky catalogue (*The Testaments Shoppe*) a poem is waiting to be teased out, is metrically drumming its fingers. The Ark, the Big Banana, surely el Numero Uno in theophanyville, the chest (or throne) (or cabinet) of the shittimwood o'erlaid of beaten gold, and with staves of the shittimwood through golden rings and thus would it be borne; and here the Presence of the Almighty of Abraham Noah and Moses dwelt, the God, the Yahweh of the mountain peaks, Talmudic, unforgiving—dwelt On High, but also here, amongst the heart of the Tribes, and spake unto His people: something like an atomic reactor, she reasons, running gung-ho on transubstance. Something like light's, or infinity's, intercom.

And so the poem might be about kitschy secularizing: the Ark as plastic pencil sharpener (pencils, then, becoming those staves on either side, their shavings filling the smokily transparent-sided central box). The Ark as Q-tips organizer, tape measure, recipe tin. She tries to work it out in half-baked notational phrases, scratched-through, arrowed, nothing going right and the day escaping into the colors of dusk: plum, and a stain like muddy cognac at the horizon.

She tries to imagine the cumbersome weight on *her* shoulders, of wood poles holding the gravid, teeming housement of the Lord of All Creation, man and woman and beast did He create, and the fires, and the firmament. Surely their vestments included substantially padded shoulders?

They consulted it, under its gryphonesque gold cherubs, in personal crisis; they paraded it onto the field of war and, lo, the enemy hosts did tremble. Even when the shield-thumping Philistines sneak the Ark away in battle and bring it unto the city of Ashdod, there the Lord smote them with emerods (this she unmurks with her dictionary: hemorrhoids), and they commanded, let the Ark be carried therefore unto Gath, but there also the Lord grew wroth, and smote, "and they in Gath were afflicted with emerods in their secret parts," and so unto Ekron (emerods again) until they did return that mighty smiter of infidel flesh, with a tribute of "five golden mice" and (how they configured it representationally she can't guess) "five golden emerods."

Okay, but what was it *really* like?—when the Pillar of Flaming and Darkness funneled back into its cube, and what was left was a kerchief's-worth of the dust of the plains, settling along with the flies on the open lips a sword tore out of a five-year-old's throat, and a mother hunkered over that useless pile whining *why* at the edge of the land of milk and honey.

She's seen that too, when the t.v. and bullhorns halted their whompwhomp adrenalin-roiling jingoism, and what remained at the side of a toppled Harley was a woman dyed in engine oil and blood. Perhaps the poem is about that lulu of a step between deific infrastructure and the pitiful wobbly table of human affairs. Whatever, the poem had better get off its spongy butt and shake its fringed tatas a little: it's night, the lid's clicked blackly down, the creeping sleepies are on her.

And what *was* in it? A voice? A bomb? The wept tear of a god it requires four men to carry? It must have been so . . . *real* then, having God under your chin like a Stradivarius strung with peeled nerve. Was God the music pouring forth? Some scholars think the Ark held a meteorite. Does God have a "soul"? Could a meteorite be God's soul, dropped like a burning nickel, to Earth?

She witnessed an autopsy once, the bric-a-brac kidneys, liver, and heart lined up on the chest like garage sale items; then what was the life-force, the spirit part: a diaphanous cockroach skittering through the shadows of those wares? What left the witches, when they salved their palms and soles with their concocted goos of elderwort and bristleroot, and flew? The poem might be about containment, about ideas of "in" and "further in," if she weren't closing her eyes now, if it all wasn't a haggis of crossed-out lines and a catalogue.

The Ark a "budvase of swirled lead crystal" . . . The Ark a "patented lock-lid airtight bagel bin" . . . The Torah Ark each synagogue has today, and the old men kissing it with their fingers, over and over, as if dipping into *poi* or *couscous*. . . . Dreams, and the Ark. Blankness, and the Ark. The chalk that draws on this blankness. The blossom, the out-of-the-body blossom, wafting out of a pulse-point on its etherically-thin but sufficient stem: nodding over her, nodding simply with weight, or with an understanding assent, it's hard to tell, but nodding, glancing over those scattered notes and nodding, *Yes, this,* and nodding, *Yes, here,* and arcing over the bed, you might say as if in the sign of a covenant.

Etruscan

"xzm'g yv ivzw yb zmb nzm li dlnzm orermt."

Oh exkyoozay*mwah:* that's code. A simple one, a = z, b = y, etc. It means Etruscan "can't be read by any man or woman living."

Sex isn't enough. If it were, if our natural skin-to-skin congruence, flutter, and juice could be the key to cryptographic empathy sufficient unto an alphabet's un-riddling, surely we *could* read these runic-looking nooses and tines inscribed around the silver cups, the ivory dice, the bronze sheep's livers with gall bladder (used for divinatory practice) of a people unashamedly given over to this same markedly carnal propulsion that drives our own small stay on the planet.

Tsk: they "do the thing," according to an outraged euphemistic Greek, "in public," and their banquets end in omnipartner, octopodish squirms. And see?—they've coupled for us in eloquent if sometimes faded murals done on marble, and especially in a terra-cotta that asks to be true to the flushes of conjugal holds. These pairs of wives and husbands stare at us with easy and voluptuary frankness through the centuries, in ways we'd *like* to think we understand: and yet the grapnels and cusps and moons and combs they've staved about their bases are a sentiment (sacred? salacious? we don't know) foreigner to our reading than animal spoor or the element-spectra of stars.

So this is the secret revealed in the days that dwindle, year-long, from the honeymoon: flesh is a separate language, and not a conductor of anything even vaguely approaching the conferral swappings of organized, public speech.

Although I know that there are ecosystems cycling invisible universe-units around, so that the elements of the periodic table are everywhere intricately mixed, I also know that the horizon of ocean and sky, to the everyday human eye, is a simpler, two-tone view: a solid layer of bluish-gray and its layer of airy meringue; the line between, the distance makes as absolute as the knock of our utterly flummoxed heads against Etruscan stone.

We all know the story in which a scribbled *dearest* is—by the finalmost narrative revelation—"really" *deadest* instead; and therefore what we try for in our own domestic powwows is to not wind up protagonists of such a plot. But the going is scarily slickery and torchless. I can turn in bed to Skyler, in the moonslaw shaved through mini-blinds: Skyler asleep, and the thought in her skull is some transistor radio bubbling the aqua patois of drowned Atlantis. Said *I love you* then kaboom, conked out. Means what? *In the civilization Skyler, stated love was often*—then garbled. Put my ear to her ear: sea sound. Slide from bed. Late. Pace.

In my study there's a book: a limestone figurine, a goddess lifted by tweezers and thread against the grain of time; we know the pollen in the petrified shit of the lady who owned this holy doll more solidly than I can guess the dream-debris of the woman beseeching me sleepily back to her side. And no, our scholars *haven't* yet deciphered the upright fish and uterine doodles and bent-back shock absorbers of the *kohau rongo rongo,* "wooden speaking boards," of Easter Island—not even the board presumably addressed to the god of the "bright field," *Rangitea;* their distress is not within our learning, nor is their surcease from that distress. And we're still stymied by the ancient script of the Indus Valley, Harappa and Mohenjo-Daro, that land the hopeless color of untreated rope. And not even these Etruscan false teeth banded with hammerworked gold, as if a barrelsmith bridged them—they may say many a poignant thing, but not in words; it's "mlgsrmt" in words (code: "nothing").

I can't even unpuzzle the language the civilization Albert was using thirty-three years back, when it invented that code with the neighboring civilization Irwin Benovitz; isolated scraps of natter blow across the ditchburn and cracked tarmac of those years, but only that. I remember the names of two warrior groups, "the cool guys" and "the creeps," and of course "tits" over and over, followed by fits of giggles.

In fact, these "hooters" are highly mysterious still, to the civilization Albert's modern science. It's a good thing, too: they say, among the other brother-and-sisterly glyphs all men and women use to texture the come-hither skin of their lives, that what we've heard inside each other, faintly, stirring at the rim of being uttered (but always fading away), are the resonatings of what we call The Gods.

They say (as always in their overly-flowery elocution) a version of this: *We come from the Anatolian steppe, the Polar drift, the Bright Field. There are signs we make, that we send through the Gates, that you see dimly. These are the Answers, these are the Thousand Answers to Things. And now we will tell you, now you shall know*

—(and then the text breaks off) and then a mote of the dust of that baked clay's breaking-off flies up a tuft of muzzy vapor where the water of the far horizon translates into the air of the far horizon, there where they lie against each other, a layer of bluish-gray and a layer of airy meringue: two bodies, all night, coupled together in darkness, whispering.

The Reliquary

is silver lilted sibilantly around an enameled urn about the size of an old-time malted shaker; supposedly the kneecap of a saint is drowsing inside its gritty celestial packing, undefeated, marmaladed in there, awaiting the Mathew Brady powder flash of Resurrection, nodding, dreaming the former glories of leper-flesh persuaded into wholeness, of the shriving scream that followed each swack of the torturer's lash.

One bitter winter day, two people accidentally meet before its second-floor museum case: the woman from my "Ark" piece, and a man from the crowd scene in "Ancient Egyptian Canopic Jars," are flimmering their first shy strands of a conversation together, the weather having ducked them separately (simultaneously) into these compliant halls, like a *shadkhen.**

Ostensibly, they have little in common. She's a poet, one of those ditsy folk whose love is fixing *pixel, lubber, rutch,* and *cresset* into the same line. He's a CPA, his columned numbers rise for him as uniformly and sturdily as if lifting the roof of the Parthenon. Nonetheless, tiny, unseen, and unspoken spondees of attraction overflow them, and while I don't want to make what my niece with her chic bored look would call "a great big effing deal" out of either lust or effluvial waves of interconnection, destiny, star charts, etc., still the hall *is* charged with heartstuff here, in what, with a title like "The Reliquary," I thought would be a religious work.

And in fact, while they make sophisticates' rarefied versions of googoo eyes, the kneecap, in its swaddling rags and pneuma, is pietistically thinking "paternoster," "noumenon," "hierophantic," and the other bodacious concepts of an orthodox devotion. The knee is remembering the hamstrings and the plaited nerves that made of it a harp's case, or a zither's, for the glorying forth of psalm and lamentation, of jeremiad and forthright dulcet praise. The knee is bent in reverie on the nave's stone floor again, the way a forehead might be lowered to tap obeisantly, once, upon the sacred ground as the great mercurochrome smear of the sun appeared and a man therefore faced East in adoration and penance.

Ah, penance—! That calcium shell is adrift in its river of reenvisioned iniquities: the singing, oops, no, the *singeing* of the nipples under the fired rods; the flail; the wheel; the bones of the fingers snapped in two like rabbit bones; the stake; the lance. . . . Adrift in doctrinal exquisitude. . . . Adrift in each of the few but madly vatic moments when someone's scaled-over eye or ulcer-pitted groin would yield to a fumbling human touch from which the healing sizzle of God Above shot electrically,

---

Yiddish, for "matchmaker"

29

like an eel; and then the blind rejoiced in sight as did the pained in the lifting of pain; and then a hush betook the crowd, in which The Word and The Way would be fulminated delightfully via a parable. . . .

All this may as well be the arcane speculation of another solar system, in the museum's contempo coffee shop. These two exchange the secret signals of love like freemasons meeting in a roomful of uninitiated slobs. The very air they sit in shines as if simonized. Look—she sees their individual coffee steams caduceus themselves around each other in erotic promise. The way she shapes her lycra! . . . How he burlily leans *into* a tough-put question, as if shoveling snow! . . .

And even so, the urn is with her: she thinks she can hear it, purring in *idle;* she thinks she can feel its transmillennial aura of ecclesiastical rapture. *That* part of her ponders away: if there *is* Resurrection, from what unguessed-at, astral-plane Goodwill shops and junktiques will the scattered skeletal units of saints be collected for reassembly? (If she rummaged those shelves would she come across, say, Van Gogh's ear in a pile of 19th-century parts, its last heard word still ticking Time inside it?) She's read of one saint's ulna saved in a vessel of gold shaped as an arm, and of a saint's skull in a head-shaped reliquary of silver; but what of one of Christ's baby teeth, that creamily-teak corn niblet of a relic? And what of "the one true relic of Jesus' circumcision," knifed off smoothly, like a sliceling of cheese?—easily a dozen of these are containered-away in "curiosa cabinets" in European cathedrals: what are *their* jars like? . . .

It's as if she wants to take that kneecap inside her, the way they say a tree will grow around, *incorporate,* the foreign object. . . . Yes, but sometimes coffee steam outweighs the smoke that rose from Joan of Arc. Outside, the snow has thinned to one white thread unraveling the hem of Heaven. They hail a cab. They nail down a few Buds. They do most everything you'll guess by now they'd do, while the relic continues turning in place, in its tatters of drear, in an absolute faith it's the embryo that the Messengers of the Final Judgment will fashion back into a man; it can no more desist from fossicking theology than a star can stop its light. Its substance *is* an Earthly, ossified version of Genesis-energy that, two Testaments back, streamed forth originally from God's mind. Maybe this *is* a religious poem—though she wakes twined with Mr. CPA, a little groggily Bud-numbed, at the base of the downslope of fine sex.

Four legs, dah-dah-dah that run in place in bed, she thinks; and, trying not to wake him, opens her bedside notebook. Scratches in it. Scratches out. She's been working all year on *Ancient Musics*—a kind of prose poem overview of *spiritus* in its endless holy masks. If only all of the *dah-dah-dah*s could be completed. . . . Then: he rouses awake with a hungry look; and, his hand on her knee,

she closes the book.

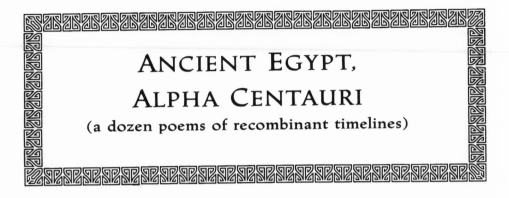

ANCIENT EGYPT, ALPHA CENTAURI

(a dozen poems of recombinant timelines)

▲

Poem Beginning with a Quote from Keith Laumer's *Galactic Odyssey* and Ending with a Quote from Mika Waltari's *The Egyptian*

Two thousand light years is a goodly distance. . . . Along the way we encountered life-forms that ranged from intelligent gnat-swarms to the titanic slumbering swamp-minds of Buroom.

And on a world that circles Ultima Three are beings
that are little more than consciousness set in a wad
of electrified jelly. On the moon of Farther Kush we find
the Master Race of maggots—if a maggot
had a scissorsy beak and the I.Q. of a physicist.
The slitherpeople of Fomalhaut mate
in the hollowed-out bowel of an enemy, and they only pray
to transitory states of matter (having, as they do,
a fear of stasis). We would be amazed especially
by the fishy cast of faces of the Spawn Folk,
with those thick-lipped gills around their throats
like coils of sentient leis, and with the tentacled
excrescences that grow forth from their heads
and are cyclically sloughed—except

that life on the ocean bottoms of Earth is equally
in this image, and Darwinianly closer
to home. The bodies seemingly all-over studded
with living rusted spikes, or swagged
in fleshy wormlike dangle-bulbs,
the blobular and ginsu-jawed and tissue-shrouded
demon fish 5,000 feet below! . . . But
really these are only logical extensions
—deeply, fittingly adapted—of the standard
range of trout and salmon and Lake Superior whitefish
that my grandfather placed on shard-ice
in the barrels of his fish store, and as well in the display case
where a few of the sharper specimens, so lushly grained
and speckled, were set like gems. He worked,

this greenhorn Jew, his sixty-hour weeks
amid an endlessness of chucked guts; there were times
when the air in the back room filled with scales
like the sky of a shook-up sno-globe,
there were times his hands were slick with so much fish
he couldn't grip the length of pipe he kept
by the great spool of twine for protection. Once,
the story goes, it slipped like a bar of bathtub soap
to his own toe, *oont I hop around der sawdust*
like a rabbit! And then: *oont a goot thing, too!*
The enemy he was ready to bop, a stranger
with a great Egyptian honker and the decidedly
"other" fashion look of Arabic dress—*this man*
become my goot frien'! In the version I know,

the immediate bonding gesture is when Wallih lifts a shnozzy
porgie up to his face in profile, and then right away
up to my grandfather's face, to indicate
they're nose-kin. I think of that
anecdote as I walk these crazy late-20th-century
fractured American streets: how we're the variations
worked upon those elements we hold in common:
pain, and pleasure; need, and need again. On Mars
it wouldn't be different; not in ancient Egypt. *The journey*
was profitable to me, for it taught me that,
if the rich and powerful are everywhere alike
and think in the same way, so also are the poor
the same the world over. Their thoughts are the same
though their customs differ and their gods bear different names.

Circa 1861

"Mother? I'm here again to freshen the water"—*lots*
of this. The radio dramatization reconstructs a typical day
in Dickinson's life, and dawdles in place a little
too slo-mo at first: this is, of course, the poet
who, in the second year of the Civil War, as every day
communiqués of victory and pomp and amputation
piled higher, wrote "The Soul selects her own Society— /
Then—shuts the Door." Behind that bolt-shot door,

however, is a viably flamboyant sensibility
the broadcast's second half enfleshes
credibly enough. Among the gentians; and over
the legendary rising terrain of her first-place bread
at the annual Cattle Show; and with a ragged fan in hand
of her notes of quirky congratulatory or condoling
words for the neighbors . . . a fierce interior blaze
is fed by this humdrummery, while

the War continues ("Yestere'en we saw a boy waltz,
his partner was a sword haft sticking halfway out his chest");
and Madame Carolista successfully ventures the highwire over Larimer Street
in Denver; and Speke is in search of the source of the Nile,
soon to stand on its banks, as herds of nsunnu and hartebeest
graze the waving nearer distance . . . but none of it
seeming to wiffle the stationary integrity of her Emily-flame
by so much as one Emily-molecule. The radio, meanwhile,

spatters at some spasm in the megahertz,
and our radio listener thinks she hears the spiritly
electrofiche sizzle of other stations zero-in on her life
for the length of that glitch. She knows they're out there
in the air, they *are* the air, some shopworn comedy and
some audience-call-in therapy-thon and music
Bach to boomboom: the twentieth century's totem name is
Simultaneity. Yes, and when she clicks the radio off

the air *remains* alive with these, she knows. Just ask
the jilted lover: aliveness isn't a function of reception.
There isn't a dime in the house that's not a silver rink
for the play of these voices. They're in every breath. They're
beaming beyond Orion, and they're on the lip of the cup,
they're on *our* lips, they do the boogaloo all night
with our neurotransmitters. Opera. Elvis. This explains moments
we feel like weeping: the news is piercing our hearts.

Because of their fossils
Leonardo understood the tops of mountains rose into light

from the mangled floor of the sea. How far
have we come every morning, from how deep away,

to dig out from the corners of our eyes
such amber fragments?

The Compasses

If the past will be seen to validate a current national image
of grandiosity, then the state will subsidize scholarly
archeological expeditions, historical research, manuscript
codecracking. And if not, then not. This is the earliest
formulation of how the state and the softer sciences
interrelate. The supersecret government project

shrinks the medical research team to under-corpuscle size
and then injects it into the subject's circulation (there
to ride the great blood rivers and micropinpoint the problem,
rooting it out completely at the subcellular level) only
if the health of a statesman or military commander
is in jeopardy; it's unthinkable they'd fund it

for the purely wonder-stuffed pleasure of learning
the body the way we'd paddlewheel up other unknown interiors,
stopping to watercolor the spigoted caverns, meditate
inside an expanse of densely webbed and brambled parkland,
dig up a tussock, sing off-key, return home with a bag
of souvenirs. If I've been describing a poem (the tweezery

exploration of a self, until we disappear inside
the poet's system like a pill) it isn't one of the Old Ones: then,
the gods stomped lightning out of the mountain, and
the poem explained their impossible, Parnassian ways
to mortals; then, the poem was many-armed and
many-faced, and spake the Verities that govern us. Now,

—well, as Howard Nemerov said, "Every poet's middle name
is Mimi." I'm here! I had grandparents! Look, I even have
a photograph of them!—much triste and joi and frisson
the size of a hatband. A poppyseed dinner roll. A condom.
A new age "healing crystal." A tear duct like an s-f
"wormhole" into alternate spacetime. This increasing

personalizing is the difference we see between the compasses
Blake etches gaping out of the Creator's hand (they *bind,*
he says, *the infinite with an eternal band*) and
the compasses Donne has stand for the love-hinged
parting of one specific couple glorying in their everyday
seventeenth-century soap opera. Don't

misunderstand me; the universe inside-outs itself
from anthrocentric to solarcentric, nations topple,
dinosaur ideas stalk the land . . .   *of course* I cherish
the counterbalancing intimacies of the small
and finely-calibrated lyric poem! Of course I love
each sesame seed and eyelash of its warbling. But

I think I was wrong, before: I think the governments
will fund that poem. Will keep its author regarding
the family album. While the iron wheel rolls imperturbably
over the hills, and the bucket-jawed scoops eat
empires out of a thousand tiny lives, and the planets
clink together inside a velvet bag on the fat hip of power.

This Needle's Tip,

that we would call infinitesimal, is
—in its "scanning electron micrograph"—the corbeled
and tunneled and buttressed and corrugate
Tower of Babel as Bruegel envisioned it under construction,
crawling with people like maggots in a busy cheese.
If only a thing would be itself, and not (as well)

its other self . . .   then I could be easy today, with the world
and its knowable definitions; with its outlines of lead
for its shapes of stained glass; with its inventory. But
always: "Hey, this Tantric zigzag-pattern gong,"
some friend is saying, and looking from his art to his job,
or his job to his art, from one cubism eye to another,

"would make a great designer hubcap." In a night
we'd all rather not have had, a friend with a little engine
of red wine revving inside her, once said that
the niceties of the nice, nice house—her hand inclusively
indicated everything from the cloisonné napkin rings
to a daughter's college fund—she'd got by whoring

a bit on the side (or "dating" for "the agency," as she put it
with a seven-ton look) but "don't tell Larry." And where
was that happy homeowner? "Ha! Which one,
Larry the Good or his Evil Twin?"—and then began the long story
of fracture and duplicity. On a night like that,
by bonfire-light, near Antwerp, Bruegel

studied the boil of revelers, as Carnival ethos,
and pots of an amber-muscled Carnival ale, unbuttoned
normalself from furtiveself, and on the grounds
prepared with a slick of pig's-grease, antic dancers
spun, their bodies turning like mill machinery
lubricated with weasel-cum and with goatslobber; and

the next day sketched his cityscape of syndics,
clerics, and herringmongers in all of their twofold
being: and so, a scooped-out egg—on legs;
a gluttonous toad with human hands; a face
all buttock (its mouth its asshole); "people," things,
you don't know where the man stops and the lizard begins,

or the duck, or the spiny boar. What seem to be
Biblical scenes are set in the sixteenth-century snows
of Flemish villages. Simple sights—a magpie, say,
or a line of stumbling men—are revealed as parables
for some didactic concept. Nothing inner is one
with its surface. Except . . . there's a corner

of brown that's almost a *reverential* brown, and here
a woman whose inch of paint is alive with concentration
shows a young boy how to mend his leather fish-pouch,
with a needle older than she is. *Here,*
she says. *Like so. Now you.* He tries, and she waits
with a patient and unaccountable goodness.

The Saga of Stupidity
and Wonder

The history of the world could be written
in anything's history: native gourds; meteor rubble;
the capping machine at bottling plant number 7 . . .
I'm convinced of this—how anything,
gripped right and studied long, contains the telescoped
story of everything, the way our protein coding holds
the germ of the lizard we once were. It's so

tempting to start the saga of stupidity and wide-eyed wonder with
us, in bed this morning, waking into another
day of our individual lives and our life together; but
any unit would do. Say . . . oh, say birds. In
1497, in Zurich, the citizens tried and
hanged for sorcery (truly) a rooster
accused of laying an egg. Or then

there's the tale Odoric of Pordenone brought back
from his travels "on the farther side of the sea.
I beheld," he tells us, a man who journeyed
with a faithful cloud of 4,000 partridges following him.
His journey was three days. When he slept, they
gathered like one solid object around him. When he walked,
they were his constant weather: the air was 8,000 wings.

Meop

1.

The scenario is: I'm six, and an invincible Venusian army of robots
swarms the city, easily conquering its human defenders with (guess what)
death rays shooting like 1954 home-movie-projector lightbeams
out of their boxy heads, in *Target Earth*. In *Devil Girl from Mars,*
the eponymous leather-fetishy siren of outer space attacks
accompanied by Chani, stomping hunk-o'-hardware robot
extraordinaire, whose particular laserlike sizzle disintegrates
a tree, a barn, a village truck, and a villager. No oratory
dissuades these invaders, no pitiable stare. And if this
somehow all sounds comic in my cavalier retelling, I
assure you it wasn't, then—no, it was set to exactly
my level of terror then: we're born instinctively knowing
an enemy awaits us, and the world provides it a series of faces
keyed to match our ageing understandings. Though there's also Tobor (robot

backwards), he of 1954's *Tobor the Great:* playpal of the movie's
plucky eleven-year-old kid-star "Gadge," and rescuer of the boy
from threatened tortures at the hands of foreign spies
(of the kind who speak like ziss, and hiss and glower).
The lesson is: of every order of being, there must be
nemesis and hero, in a tug-of-warring balance. Satan
predicates St. Michael, and vice versa: they
require one another. Yes, but how to tell? The neighbor-lady
led away one afternoon by a county official
for holding her daughter's open palm against the flat of an iron
"so she'd listen good . . ." spoke not one hokey ziss or zat to flag
her culpability. I knew about the moon's dark side:
aliens' secret bases were there. But what about people?
—what about *in*side? what about simple earthly night?

2.

The fabled Kansas flatness seems to go so far, we *couldn't*
be the same "us" by the time we've finally exited its distance.
When I drive this wheaten vastity, I see how life is space
enough for each of us to segue through a programmed range
of consecutive selves, some less than what we'd wish for, some
so seemingly "other" we shiver in our passage. And that Shiva
the Destroyer, and Shiva the Dancer of Life, are one—is just
a mythic hyperstatement of whatever robot/tobor me-*du-jour* we
carry confusingly into the lives of those we love (see
Paramount's 1958 *I Married a Monster from Outer Space*).
My wife's in bed tonight with a novel in which one brother becomes
a ruthless mafioso, one a priest. And then she sleeps,
whoever she is in her recombinant life, while I'm up
writing, whoever I am. Sometimes I think of Skyler

and myself: a car is driving through the lengthways Kansas landscape
like some blip on an ongoing medical readout, everyone hoping
it stays within the central "steady-state" for soma
and psyche, but sometimes it peaks off toward the edges.
Then, whatever (even ordinary) patience we can summon
is required; or it thins into ire; or infrastructures itself
into something amazingly like forgiveness. Just last night
I turned in bed to see us both awash in moonlight
made so jittered by the stir of nearby trees, it looked
as if we gave off semaphore—although the message
might have come from Alpha Centauri, for all I understood it.
Her face went visible, then guarded; clear, then variegated
weirdly. All night, both of us: a flickered glimpse of beings
from the lunar dark side. Trebla. Relyks.

In science fiction, in a giant glass tube the size of a body,
they freeze a body. On Planet X it thaws. He's alive. 100
years have passed and he's alive and 22. He remembers
a story: they send a man faster than light. FTL-drive, it's
called in that story. And when he returns, the people who live
by Earth's speeds are his grandchildren. 22, and he has grandchildren.
He remembers a story: once they had something called photographs,
they froze you in light. The other you went on, dying.

The Lives of the—Wha'?

[The painter] Rosa Bonheur . . . visited abattoirs and markets dressed as a man in order to gain knowledge.

—Kenneth Clarke

No punishment deterred her
trousered stirring-in with the regulars,
greedily memorizing everything: a stink
so solid you'd think you could slather
gesso across it; the trim, particular loveliness
of interserried muscle,
on the rib-meat of some halved and hoisted ox;
the pile up to her waist
of its hawserly, coiled gut. No fine,
no forced confinement, halted this
determined incognitowork. And even more,
I like Vasari's stories of devotion

so intently rapt, the world itself
floats off unminded—of Paolo Uccello,
whose wife chides "Come to bed," but he replies "Oh,
what a lovely thing is this perspective!" wakeful
while the rest of the fifteenth century snoozes,
ceaselessly diminishing the hare and the waled field
and the greave or the helmet dropped in battle, down
his lines to the vanishing point. "Secluded for months
. . . without ever pausing a moment," says Vasari. Feet
lumped up in a bucket of cedar shavings—keeping them warm
all night without a need to leave the easel.
The lives—the singular, undivertable

46

lives of the artists!—this is my theme. And they're not alone.
". . . the rest of the fifteenth century snoozes"—wrong. While
Paolo oversees his distances, the sea lords
of this Age of Exploration trace *their* (mercantile) way down lines
—mercator lines; perhaps there's a culturovisionary
connection, suddenly paintings and empires equally
seek horizon. Not that home is ever devoid of delight
or horror, of course, but something in farness
vivifies such concepts; scenes of airborne turquoise streams
of Birds of Paradise, or scenes of roof-hung
human ribs in a smokehouse. This is the Age
when even Heaven opens up to a perspectivist's

geometry; where formerly the Afterlife was sere,
and acorporeally devotional, now couples (say,
like the parallel lines of a landscape, if one takes them
far enough) are reunited: in Elysium,
in the fields of Everlasting: and the precedential
dead are shown in poems and paintings
welcoming their late-arrival spouses to a physically continued
matrimony. One monk, Celso Maffei (1425–1508),
gets funky, claiming that "the body of the lowest saint
will there taste fifty times more sweet than honey,
another saint a hundred times, a third a thousand."
Sign me up, guy! Speaking of saints, did you know

—huh? My wife steps into this poem now,
asking me why I always sneak off in disguise
to a secret place in my head when she's trying
"to have a serious conversation" (read here: money,
laundry, relatives, the cavalier disdain of Time
for the wood of a house). "Disguise"? Did you know
Rosa Bonheur worked her hair
into a cart-man's cap when she needed the spike-tipped,
right-there stench of the abattoir in her nostrils?
—how this poem began. We're *made* of electric
infinitycrackle that won't stop branching forth until
the brain is as large as the universe. Yes,

but then there's Michelangelo's more
obsessively-focused example, on his back
all day to paint the Chapel's ceiling, then by night
again, "in a hat of folded paper with a candle on it
burning over his head, so that in this way
he could see, and have his hands free." This
he cared about, and little else, and when
he would remove his dogskin leggings after sometimes months
of living in his clothes, "his skin came off as well."
The lives of the artists. The prices of beauty.
The stern but ecstatic intensity of the one thing
loved into beauty. In his *Resurrection* fresco

this emerges as those famous wakened bodies
that are packed with the symmetrically sculpted vitality
of panthers. Human panthers—it's the soul's light
breaking through them. We can imagine
a living umbilicus of bodies spiraling up from Earth
to gather on this Higher Plane, to meet
at this forever-point—and we can see them
rising out of the S-curve rows of the fields,
and out of the corner bars still holding
cool brown bottles by the neck, and jiving,
weeping, giving grand high-fives, and wives
reclaiming husbands here, and husbands greeting wives.

Own Recognizable

They bound the foot—they shriveled it like a salted persimmon
first, to specification, then fit it into its slipper.
Alien, to us: there are planets in science fiction more familiar.
And yet they wrote *The white plate is broken, now is the time
of the yellow plate*—of summer, they meant, our own
recognizable summer. And elsewhere they mummified
nine thousand temple cats in a burial shaft, and
elsewhere slit the penis skin at puberty and sewed
a jangling bell inside, but everywhere *The seasons turn
like a pot on a wheel, my roebuck, my Nile flower.* I
was watching you sleep. How far were you? If the animal brain
is far, if gender is far, then astrophysics couldn't measure it,
not in human words. You woke, you said *Listen: I had
a dream. We were two birds on one branch, singing.*

What the Poem
Is Actually About

In an earlier part of "I Used to Think So" a female is alluded to:

As she leaves,
and the door jerks to a close,
I listen hard into the stillness,
into the building's actual weather,

hearing nothing that loves me,

as if each detail
had to be tricked into meaning.

. . . The "she" here is not referred to before the single line containing her
pronoun and is never referred to again . . . the poem is not going to tell
us the story; Dana has deliberately suppressed it. . . . While such an
exercise might be amusing, it is not helpful in determining what the poem
is actually about.

—from a review of Robert Dana,
by Fred Chappell (*Georgia Review*)

1. An Epistolary History of the Seventeenth Century

Woman Writing a Letter (Gerard Terborch) about 1654
Young Woman Reading a Letter (Jan Vermeer) about 1658
Man Writing a Letter (Gabriel Metsu) no date given
Woman Reading a Letter (Gerard Terborch) 1662
Girl in Blue Reading a Letter (Jan Vermeer) about 1665
The Love Letter (Jan Vermeer) about 1669
Lady Writing a Letter (Jan Vermeer) about 1670
Interior with a Young Woman Reading a Letter (Pieter de Hooch) no date given

2. Swearing to Light

There are clues—there are a few clues
to the contents. Here, a mandolin
is leaned against the spinet: she's awaiting
her "accompaniest," her lover. Or here, on the wall
above the head of this deeply concentrating young man
is a painting in which a three-mast vessel is lost like a fly
between two hands of wild gray-green water: so, his
stormy love (or financial?) affairs, etc. A woman
posed beside a snuffed-out candle. A woman
stroking the languorous sheen of the cat in her lap.
But these, at best, are guesses. What the letters say
—the letters being heavily composed here, or unfolded and read,
and fussed with, creased and recreased, then
unfolded and then read again—these letters slyly angled
in the Netherlandish light so that they gleam like risen cream
amid the shadows . . .   what they *truly* say
we'll never know, and by this given secrecy
they gain their mysterious power. Once you see this,
you can yield to the itchy pleasure of being in a room
with the inviolate. Once you understand this,
you can understand how art is most like life
when it includes what won't abandon its every integrity
to confession. And—
                              if you *don't* understand? . . .
In *Girl in Blue Reading a Letter,* surely
she's pregnant?—and the wall-map,
done in sun-touched umber-golds the shade of fresh crusts
—someone's away, yes?—a mariner, maybe.
But all we can swear incontrovertibly to
is the light, the glorious pour of light
around this woman and the letter that she holds
and reads with such a great intensity
the paper and her face create a field of charge
between them . . .   yes, the light, the color

a pearl would breathe if a pearl could breathe,
the light that wipes the moment clean of facts
and free of history . . .
while in another room of the world, some reviewer
stumbles through darkness.

3. Last Night in Bed,

full anger fills our half-sleep.
We'd twist any way, to not touch.
Our perimeters of privacy, exquisite
to the sixteenth-inch, are ably defined
and dextrously defended—knee-jut,
elbow-wangle—even through the near-doze
of our consciousness. Today,
the same: enormous, if invisible,
architectural fancies—emotional
moats and palisades. We'll go
to any lengths for this
securing of personal boundary: Louis XV,
seeking safety from the everpresent buzz of his own servitors,
hid in royal chambers intimately mazed by secret passages
and concealed stairways—and,
for his hunting lodge at Choisy, had constructed
a mechanism that raised a fully set table into the dining room
from the kitchen below, then lowered the gutted table
at meal's end, without the need
of in-person attendance: I imagine it
elaborately clanking like the wheels of some *deus ex machina*
winched in for its lines and then winched out again.
But the units of privatization
needn't be so hugely engineered. Carlyle
recounts a splashy, sententious literary evening: "Dinner
was large, luminous, sumptuous . . ." and
". . . there reigned in all quarters a cackle as of Babel."
Then "I looked up"—there "sate Wordsworth,
silent, slowly but steadily
gnawing some portion of what I judged to be raisins,
with his eye and attention placidly fixed
on these and these alone."

4. As Long as I'm Quoting,

here's a postcard (June 9, 1916)
that I found in a memorabilia store.

> "Dear Emily:

I am afraid I shall not get what I came for.
But shall stay on a few days more
in hopes. All OK.

> Love to All, J."

This, in a spidery sepia script.
I don't know what it "means"—that is, its referents
elude me, in their nearly eighty years of occluding events—
and yet this message has always seemed to speak with eloquence
for my life, and for the lives of my friends.

5. The "She" Here

I jerked the door closed.
Let him listen into the stillness,
I thought. Then I was out in the boomboom noise
of traffic-blather, jackhammer, wolf-whistle,
all of the zoo-cacophony, all of the planets
skillfully turning their corners on one wheel
—out in the world, myself, responsive to its winds
like something fletched. Oh, there are times
a woman needs to hear the murmurs of monogamy
come lazing up her camisole: "You're butter
down there, baby," he'd say, and lick his longest finger
slick in proof. There are times when a woman will say
the corresponding sentiment back, and mean it, and
stretch contentedly in the contented hammock rocking
of Greenfield, Iowa. And there are the other times.
I left. I jerked the door closed.
I stormed out of the building's actual weather.
I traded it for that butterfly wing
they always say in chaos theory is causing a typhoon
in Siam or among the Spice Islands. I wanted
their little lacquered beakers of musk unstoppered and poured
along the crooks of my knees, I longed for
—what? I couldn't really say,
a scorch, an I.V. drip from the want jar.
If I knew, I still wouldn't tell you—it's a uniform
in size *me* that I needed trying on, and no one else
is allowed at the mirror
while those laces and snaps are adjusted. And
the thing I broke to get here—? the glittery
sherds in a furrow in Greenfield, Iowa—?
That's Atlantis, now. That's under
so much ocean it's Saturn now, it's Alpha Centauri now.
I'll tell you this: in every one
of what we call "relationships," there's one last thing
that can never be said. Well I said it.
It's enough you know what yours is,

I won't tell you ours. The light would shrink
from words like that, like antimatter.
The rest of it you know, though:
I took three deep breaths and closed the door,
and clicked my heels like teletype down the tile hall
and into the crickets and highway-moan and hubbahubba,
and disappeared into the August night,
butter on a griddle.

Real Speeches

The Child is Father of the Man
                    —William Wordsworth

"Applying for the mortgage loan is inimical
to the poetic imagination," Coleridge says
somewhere, as he sits in patient, ursine contemplation
of the tinder glimmering lower in the fireplace, in a world
so far removed from verification of charge card balance
(or even from velcro), that its sea-tint crystal inkwells
and bills of Parliament and reticules may as well be rockjut
slathered over by trilobites in the Devonian ooze.
This makes it more amazing that Coleridge's insight zips
unerringly to its future-century target: "The poetical fancy
exists inversely to any interior process undertaken by
the pecuniary and slimy," or words to that effect, I'm sure
of this, although I remember that Wordsworth rushes in
just then, his alpenstock held overhead
like a megalomaniac conductor's baton, and cogently argues that
"a poetry desirous of incorporating the real speech of real men
must therefore" (and everyone loves the dingy floss of his hair
and deepening apoplectic pink of his forehead) "incorporate even
the reptilian prattle of pinchpenny beancounter branch-bank
credit officers in their neutral-upholstered decor,"
I know I've read that in the preface to *Lyrical Ballads,*
or a version of that. Then Wordsworth, still expatiating,
insistently tugs at his friend's great rumpled sleeve,
and leads him over the leas and the moors and the downs
and the dales and vales and dingles, as set
as a squire's best-trained pointer on bringing Coleridge
to the one place that he knows of, where the poets
and the CPA's of our con- and involuted "human condition"
most readily mingle in an easy mutuality
—and he'll morph them both through time if necessary,
he so loves to make his point.
At McDonald's at 8 in the morning, *every* morning,

the widowers club convenes: Eddie Tummy,
Wholesale Sam, Bad Bridge Job Sid, and The Other Sam,
four coffees and four bland danishes no matter *what*
meltdown horseshit heat (the term is Eddie Tummy's) or knee-high
winter snow the weather brings. The famous speed of light
and the value of pi are no more constant
than this foursquare klatch of which, in *some*
mythology no doubt, the whole of the universe is borne
without a wobble from its first explosive yawn
unto its final chilly fizzle. Even here,
amid the wadded wrappers—even here, with the mother smacking
her stone-faced child (drowned out by the blare of the horns)—
a rightness happens, shapeliness occurs,
if the daily pattern of four men kvetching,
shaggy-dogging, and in general tower-of-babeling the b.s.
in a shared aesthetic is shapeliness. *I'm* lost
in the moneygibberish application form for the mortgage loan and a thick
Sargasso coffee mist, and by the time I look up,
Coleridge and Wordsworth have already joined these four,
the formermost having splurted Wholesale Sam and Eddie Tummy
with a novice's squeeze of his ketchup packet,
entirely missing the amber plaque of his hash browns
—I can see he takes a barely suppressible pleasure in this
tomfoolery, and would like to include Bad Bridge Job Sid
in a second (and intentional) bombardment. Wordsworth
peckishly frowns. The Other Sam says, "Boobeleh,
kiss my *a!* This cocksucker nebbish they call a President
can mouth about his 'trickledown prosperity' until the moon
is as blue as Sidney's balls, but I'm tellin ya" (now
he deftly orchestrates his lingo with his plastic coffee swizzler)
"you and me ain't gonna see diddlysquat come tricklin."
Eddie Tummy begins a rebuttal around a bite of scrambled eggs,
"Look, Mr. Economist Schmuck—" and it seems to me
that Wordsworth isn't as pleased with these exempla of his
as he'd planned: he likes to think about the rabble,
in their uncouth bumpkin way, decrying the florid excesses
of monarchy, but *this* unseemly convening is so . . .   he
looks at Coleridge. Coleridge is absorbed

in eking grins from the smacked-around kid at the opposite table
(mommy having slipped to the john) by demonstrating his sudden
mastery of that very challenging instrument,
the ketchup geyser. "Ooo," the kid says.
"Nebbish! Nebbish!" says Coleridge back. ". . . and clamp
their Congressional lips," says Eddie Tummy, "around your wallet
like a putz, and suck your blood straight out." I *believe*
it's disapproval I see claiming Wordsworth's face, but it's
maybe dyspepsia: I've also tried the sausages
from time to time. "Ker-smish!" says Coleridge.
"Hey! *You!*" says the mother on returning. Now The Other Sam
is reminded by this frolic that he's promised to bring
the latest Happy Meal toy to his granddaughter, who
he loves so much he carries her googoo face around (in a mystical way)
in his pacemaker, as some others would a loved one in a locket
—he's up at the counter now, conniving a secret decoder
out of a register boy who's sure he shouldn't have to bother
with Happy Meal (i.e., burger or Chicken McNugget) requests
in the middle of breakfast trade. "You guys—I'm gonna go
put this in my car." "Why, it's so precious? Okay, go."
Yes, it's so precious. Out in the morning sun he's suddenly
out in the morning sun of 1931—he's five, he's standing there
with one hand, as small as a penny is how it feels, in his mother's hand;
in his other he grips his Little Orphan Annie Club Decoder,
not unlike this later model but metal, *real* metal, not a crummy
acid-yellow plastic. *Everything* then was more substantial, yes?
The pie safe in a restaurant looked as solid as an ocean tanker.
Marriages lasted. Nickels could be saved and mean a new home.
Not like now, some dummy sitting in there with his stinking
home loan paperwork and a nickel-diameter ulcer.
Back then—morning sun. His mother wets a twist
of cotton napkin in her mouth and swabs a small smudge from his cheek.
They're off to visit Tantë Mahlke—mommy's mommy's sister,
they tell him. She's sick. She smells like unwashed laundry, unwashed feet.
He was scared. He sat there, as the grownups babbled, determinedly
entrancing himself with the circular deco design of the decoder,
falling into it, as if it were a hypnotist's disc, and willing himself
away from these enormities, to another plane of being. Unaccountably,

he's scared *now:* 1995. He does it still—he'll lose himself
in the overdetailed workaday plot of "police procedural" novels,
Sid or Eddie will need to dig him out by force. "I guess,"
he says, "that the kid I was is the father
of who I've become," or words to that effect, I'm sure he says this,
near the drive-thru lane, abidingly somewhere inside.

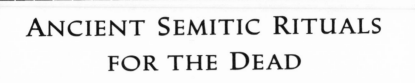

ANCIENT SEMITIC RITUALS
FOR THE DEAD

1.

Those who live on the earth—between the upper and lower worlds—may call on the residents of either level to help them with their earthly problems.
—McDannell & Lang

I'm with Thick, who supplies the lithe waitpeople of The Guzzling Hole
their weekly grade-A grass, so in return our Coronas are free (and
we'd eased slickly into parking marked MANAGEMENT ONLY). Let me
correct myself: all beers have a price. Tonight, mine's being the ear
down which Thick's weighty sadness funnels.
If you slyly check the faces, half the patrons here slug beer that's
similarly dearly-purchased. Sadness; listening to sadness—these
may be our commonest coin.
                    It makes the barlight seem to gleam
especially poignantly: on stein rims, pendants, gold hoop earrings,
scattered in the air—the constellation *Melancholia*. Maybe,
I think, like the actual stars, these need the proper background
darkness, to be seen. That's us. That's people, alright.
That's each of our swizzled stories.
                    Thick's begins
of course with a woman of course, a looker, a goddess, a bitch;
whatever hardness he had to his heart, filleted in an instant.
Then (beer five) the maudlinesque: although she's gone,
he has a pair of her (but do I *want* to know this?) smoky hose
he still lets spin around the dryer
with his own clothes, like a ghost of sexual frolic,
etc. Before long, even the lady lawyers
standing at the rail are moved:
                    one level below
this romantic complaint, his mother is dying a year ago
of ovarian cancer, a tumor the size of a coffee mug, is dying
with various guilts still and forever knotted inside her: this is
six months after his father's death,
a freak electrical accident on the riveting line,
                    and I'm
murkbrained, remembering my only hands-on novice attempt

63

at microscope work (in junior high): resolving
ever-further levels up from blur to focus.
                                        And
I'll tell you this about body weight: I'm thin,
my seventh beer has brought me deeper, quicker. *My* father
is also dead, and I'm down to the elemental
minus-signs of grief, the argon and nitrogen of woefulness,
the cinching ring of trauma we exit in being born,
the slathering worm, the eerie singing from out of the medulla oblongata,
I'm there in the ash and the lime of the soil
already, waiting for Thick and five or six others
to join me in imploring the dead, in wringing out
some sub-omega word for them to respond to. . . .
                                        When I know
again what's happening, it's 2 a.m. We're out in the lot,
the imbibery locking up behind us. Thick is whispering
fervently to the sky, is pounding his fists at the sky
as if it were sheet-tin thundering back. This lamentation
and jeremiad know no bounds, for verily the bitterroot
and the gall and the sting are given unto endlessness,
from micro to macro, from Heaven to Sheol
—such is the enormity of distress
here, on the middle plane.

2.

The veneration of ancestors assumed organized ritual forms. In one such ritual the participants consumed large quantities of wine and poured out wine for the dead.

—McDannell & Lang

Time: the late 1980s.
A bare stage, softly lit in the center,
and dimming at either side.

From offstage left:	*A few moments later, then continuing*
a 1940s tavern song	*simultaneously, from offstage right:*
on banjo or accordion.	*a 1980s rock tune on boozing (say,*
	"Glory Days" by Springsteen).

(A man, late thirtysomething, walks in from stage right, to center stage. He's carrying a gleaming uncapped half-gallon of Mogen David wine and two glasses. He's a bit wobbly: to get this far, he's required a night of Coronas.)

Son: Father?   (unsure of the ritual formula)

(no response)

Son: Father, it's Albert.   (pause)   Albert, the son of Irving.   (pause)   Avram ben Yitzchak.

Voice: (the voice speaks from offstage left)   Albie?

Son: (surprised at both the voice's timely appearance and the use of his childhood pet name)   Yes—"Albie."

Voice: Auntie Hannah always called you Albie—   (as if continuing a conversation from only moments earlier)

Son: Auntie Hannah always called me Albie—

Voice: —when you were a little boy.

Son: —when I was a little boy.

Voice: She said that you had—

Son: —"bedroom eyes." She said that I had "bedroom eyes." And—

Voice: —and that you were as smart—

Son: —and that I was as smart as a major! (He speaks more easily now; he remembers that conversation among the living is almost always also a matter of repeated ritual formulae; and so this serves as a bridge to our talk with the dead.)

Voice: How's she doing? The cough—?

Son: She's fine. (though clearly he's not certain of this) Hannah— (formalizing it, especially for the occasion) —Your sister is fine.

Voice: And Mommy. (It's more a statement than a question: he can't imagine his wife as managing fully capably without him, and yet his love won't allow his imagining her as anything less than content.)

Son: Yes, fine. We're all fine. (feeling pleased to report this news, yet somehow guilty for having reached this state of affairs without his company) And Livia and The Boog are okay, Lindsay's in second grade, and Ian . . .

Voice: Ian?

Son: Livia had another child, Daddy (aware of his slipping from "Father" now that the subject is come to parenthood and everything feels softened) —a boy. She named him after you: Ian.

Voice: Ian? "Irving" is "Ian"?

Son: They're all fine. And—I'm married again.

Voice: I don't see how "Ian" is "Irving." Albie, *you're* the professor; do you see?

Son: (slightly peeved at the reception of his own news) Look, believe me, "Ian" *is* the "Irving" of the eighties.

Voice: Is she good to you?

Son: (a little surprised at the reraveled conversational thread, then smiling at the question a father *would* ask, *did* ask, already seeing the next two questions forming) Yeah, yeah: good to me. Of course.

Voice: Is she pretty?

Son: (smiling at something secret—at maybe a special beauty he finds in his wife; or at the thought that his mother, his shrunken birdlike 72-year-old mother, was a beauty once, to *this* man; or at maybe simply the bonding that discussion of female good looks gives to two men, even across this greatest chasm) Pretty, you know, pretty for me. A redhead. Very smart, (he feels he should add) talented. Skyler. Skyler Lovelace.

Voice: A pretty name. (but it makes him suspicious) Albie, is she—

Son: (the second of the expected questions) —Jewish? No.

Voice: (pause) Well, Morgan wasn't Jewish. (meaning: he's used to it now) Yeah, yeah, "Morgan"—right? I remember your wedding with Morgan. Not in a *shul*—

Son: At the university.

Voice: —but you asked me, would I recite the *kiddush?* Over a *kiddush*-cup of wine. Did I sing! (he begins that ritual prayer with a soulful, heartfelt, buttery flutter in his voice, *Baruch atah adonai,* but breaks off coughing) Here (feels sheepish, as if he's let someone down) it's so dry. It's very dry, here.

Son: Look: I have the answer. (delighted that circumstance smooths the way for his offer; he pours them each a glass, then carries his father's just a bit offstage and returns to center stage)

Voice: Albie, Albie . . . thank you. (sips—sips more) It's *goooood.* (remembering *why* this commonplace wine is so good) It's so dry here.

Son: (has finished his also, pours and downs a second glass in a gulp, then walks with his wobble over to stage left, as before, and leaves the entire bottle there for his father)   It's yours.   (a little embarrassed: is it purely generosity? is it partly in petition for spectral aid or solace? etc.)   It's a gift.

Voice: Sure, boychick. You know how they say? *Foon nemen vehrt nit orem,* from taking you don't get poor.   (more sips)   You come to visit me this way, Albie, even here with the dust and the rags, I'm a rich man.   (now remembering their relationship)   But Albie—you don't drink, right? You don't get *shikker?* A little, yes, for the voice or the courage. But not to drink and drive, right?

Son: (rolling his eyes: will he die one day, himself, in another forty years, still being sixteen?—as if he *were* sixteen, his response is truculently mumbled)   Mm-hm. "Not to drink and drive."

Voice: Okay, you roll your eyes, you make your fists in your pockets, I say this because I LOVE YOU. One day I'll be gone, THEN you'll appreciate me.   (an awkward silence—saying this, he remembers he *is* gone; both of them are stunned for a moment; the father is first to recover, perhaps his strength is greater, perhaps the wine in front of him promises a clue to the easiest silence-breaker)   And the *kiddush* each year at Passover! You remember the songs?

Son: A little.   (still abashed at the drinking-and-driving speech, and thus a bit reluctant to admit he remembers the ritual holiday melodies)

Voice: A little, a shmittle. You go to *shul,* ever?

Son: No.   (not so abashed that this naked syllable doesn't cause him embarrassed discomfort)

Voice: No—but you remember.   (starts singing, sipping and singing)   *Déi-déi-yaynoo, o déi-déiyaynoo, o*

Son: (joins him)

Together: déi-déiyaynoo, *DEIYÁYNOO DEIYAYNOOÓOO,* hey! (both of them, tipsy, nostalgic, really *into it* now, increasingly merry) Sooo . . . *Eeloo hōtzee, hōtzeeyawnoo, hōtzeeyawnoo meemitzrahyim, meemitzrahyim, hōtzeeyawnoo, DÉIYAYNOO.* Sooo . . . (son realizes he's started the second verse alone)

Voice: (with the cunning but warm camaraderie of wineliness) So tell me . . . you drink with the ladies? (pause) Hey, Mr. Professor, I'm *winking* at you!

Son: Oh, right . . . right. Winking, right. The ladies. Yes, sure. We, uh, never talked about the ladies very much, you and me, you know?

Voice: Talk, shmalk. You're a *man* now! (really feeling the wine, as well as affectionate male bonding) Drinks are good with the ladies, the laughing, the hoohoohoo! (eternally the father, however) Not too much drink, though, and some of these ladies you're bragging about—

Son: (huh? he *was?*)

Voice: —be careful! *Far guteh nekht hot min shlechte teg,* From good nights you get bad days. Your old man knows, so listen (humming some snatch of tune in the middle, likely a popular dance-tune from his day) *Az der pots shteyt ligt der seychl in dr'erd,* When the prick rises up, good sense lies down. (waits) I'm WINKING! (hums more, it segues back into the Passover song from earlier, and after a while the son joins in again; he sits, a sprawling kind of sit; together they fondly hum their way, each lost in a world of reverie, through three or four more verses of *Deiyaynoo;* when they stop, they're both chuckling)

Voice: One Passover, you remember? Cousin Danny lost his spectacles—

Son: —in the tureen of chicken soup!

Voice: Yeah, yeah! "Tureen"?

Son: The pot, the big pot!

Voice: Yeah, chicken, chicken! Another Passover, you remember Mommy (laughing throughout this) got drunk a *bissel,* she IMITATED a chicken, all around the table, p-chawk, p-chawk, p-chawk!

69

Both: (laughing giddily)

Voice: And one Passover—   (stops; a new memory flashing over him)

Son: (stops laughing abruptly; intuits something)

Voice: —one Passover you were bad, you   (searching the right word)   you *rebelled,* you wouldn't join in the songs, you didn't say *amen* after the prayers, you just sat there—

Son: No, I—

Voice: —sat there and stared, you   (searching again)   you *fumed.*   (his tone is not accusatory so much as simply, tenderly, sad)   All year we'd been arguing, yes? And now this. You didn't answer *amen* a final time, I cried, do you remember?

Son: (he remembers; he can only nod)

Voice: I wept. I'd never wept in front of your mother before, this time I wept. And you came around to the head of the table, Albie—

Son: (is quietly sobbing)

Voice: —you held my head. You cradled my head, like I was a baby, you rocked me. Everybody watched, and you rocked me.

Both: (are silent a moment)

Voice: You rocked me. . . . Sleepy, yes? The wine makes you sleepy. . . . After the Passover *seder,* a nap is good.   (hums drunkenly, drowsily)

Son: Wait! Irv!   (stands)   I have questions.

Voice: (out of the drowse for a second)   "Irv"? Oh, yes.   (remembering)   Questions.

Son: About . . . well, what is it like, and what do you know now, and . . .   (trails off—it sounds so foolish, spoken aloud)

Voice: Yeah, yeah, all this I'll tell you. (humming again)   Next time, I'll tell you. *Der seych'l fort of oksn,* Wisdom travels by oxen. Slow . . . very slow. . . . One thing, though.

Son: Yes?

Voice: Albie—

Son: I'm here.

Voice: —you don't drink and then drive, boychick, okay?

Son: (an ironic silence)

Voice: Look, maybe you drink a *little.* This "Skylady"—

Son: Skyler?

Voice: —you drink a little, you hoohoohoo with her. You hoohoohoo with her for *me.* Over here, it's very dry over here. Okay now. *Ariverdairchee.*

Son: But—

Voice: Gone.

Son: But—

(no response; the light at stage left completely goes out)

Son: (speaks softly; he's speaking to himself and, as he does, he sets his empty wine glass onto the stage beside him; this now, said like a revelation)   "I'll be gone . . ."   (long pause)   "You'll appreciate me . . ."

(he's still for a moment, then lifts his foot and smashes the wine glass, quickly, cleanly, with one stomp)

(the whole stage in darkness)

—CURTAIN—

3.

Although our knowledge of this early stratum of Semitic thought is sketchy, we can see a shadowy afterlife where the status of the dead depends on the veneration of the living, and the state of the living may be influenced by the inhabitants of the netherworld.

—McDannell & Lang

The dead are weird, man—*weird.*

You know those earliest films of D. W. Griffith's?—audiences unused to the possibilities of the camera saw a close-up for the first time zeroing-in on a face, and panicked. "It looked to them," as Laurie Sheck says, "like pieces of hacked-up people there on the screen, horrible, fragmented, grotesque."

Presumably, a long shot was as disaffecting: say, a glen in foggy distance and wayfarers seemingly inches high. The logic of it would have been lost on an audience used to their own kind, live, on stage. But the actors and actresses of film *aren't* live in the usual sense—though they walk the earth, and make their speeches, and wind up playing our nervous systems like harps.

The dead are that to us. They mutterwhirl like gerbil wheels, madly, in the backs of our minds; or glide from attics, in all of their translucent *hauteur;* or drape like clammy stoles around our shoulders in moments of crisis, stoles appearing from the ectosphere, providing inexplicable wisdoms. . . . The dead and their glory. The dead and their fungal rot.

Whatever they are, they wend our world in parts, and even those parts are never fully comprehensible. Here we are in dimension *this.* It's a quality of dimension *this:* the populace of dimension *that* is too close; or too far; too other; too little like us; too much for comfort.

▲

The dead in their packed assembly hall, the filibustering dead.

They clamor. They keep on intruding and uttering their sententious opinions—though these may finally appear to *our* world as the mussing-up of a coverlet by the breeze.

They keep on sending their most exquisite hollow-eyed orators—though their language is train-moan and guttering flame. Their language: its diacritical marks are the dust motes inside rain.

. . . But over time we accustom ourselves—in time enough, with earned avidity—to the out-of-scale figures up on the screen. This really *is* "the birth of a nation," of a citizenry coeval with our own. The loves and traumas of the movie stars, their glitzy adjunct presence at political rallies, their product endorsements, their overblown talk-show dither. . . . Sometimes we live through them.

The dead. We nest our ears against their lumps of interment, seeking advice. We bring our offering-bowls of rice and our loaded panniers of flowers. We introduce them to our therapists, "I've brought Dead A and Dead Z today, I'd like you to get to know one another. . . ." Dracula rising. Hamlet and the ghost. Some days the ouija board is clearer of interference than the long-distance call. We've learned to practice necroappeasement. "Appeaseiotomy," one friend said, as she lit the memorial candle.

▲

Elephants have been known to lift the bones of other elephants killed by poachers, and to carry them long distances in a stately gait. From far, it might look as if they were bearing the columns for a Roman villa, over dusty miles to the construction site; but closer, and it looks as if the eyes in those vast seamed faces are truly doleful. Reliable sources have repeatedly seen them covering fellow elephants' corpses in gently deposited scatters of grass, or visiting the skeletons of their dead, at dusk, and defecating "copiously beside them." Commemoration.

At the death of one of the Botgate (of the south of the mountainous island Malekula) the body is covered in leaves, then set on a wooden platform at the dancing ground. It remains there for months; at the chosen moment, the head is pulled off, the scalp and hair are exactingly cut away, and the skull is put in an anthill for insects to work to a clean, unhampered white-yellow.

This is only the beginning. A life-size effigy, a *rambaramp,* of the dead man is constructed of bamboo and leaves—the skull is "fleshed out" from a vegetable paste that's sculpted into as faithfully-specific a face as possible, and properly placed atop the body. The figure is given the dead man's armlets and legbands. Then the original hair is pasted back to the cranium with the sap of a breadfruit tree. For days, this substitute-person is honored: danced around, and offered yams and slaughtered pigs. A mighty, a very mighty, celebration.

You've heard the stories: coffins replete with color teevees and miniature wet bars—as if maybe we think the great-great-great-grand-deities-to-the-*nth* of ancient Egypt were partying yet in their Eternal Lotus Fields, impatiently waiting for replenishments. We court the dead, we honor the dead, our days and nights are coefficient with theirs, and every moment of menstrual slough, lost tooth, or slept-on-and-forgotten poem reminds us of the small and daily deaths that are our preparation for taking our place amongst them.

▲

We *need* the dead. Oh sure: "the dead, the dead, the dead," blah blah, that smelly mucilloid ooze in the ground. But call those corpses "ancestry," and—ah! If they were pashas for whom the commoners balanced grapefruits on top of noodles all afternoon—then *we're* descendants of those pashas, and their elegance becomes us. Or if they were slaves, if they suffered the overseer's lash, if they stumbled under their burden of stone—then reparation is *ours,* and endless righteous indignation, and the special pleasures of redress sought. The dead are our excuse. The dead are guardians of acumen and power beyond our mortal ken.

And the dead need *us,* as the gods require our constant, perfect credulousness. Without us, what would it mean, to be an apocalyptic presence in the gray rain?—where would the spirit-tendril catch and feed?

I remember my seventh-grade science textbook: a page for *the nitrogen cycle,* arrows circling from soil to sky as surely as crumpled twenty-dollar bills were circling through Chicago all around me, to the alderman, and through the marble hallways of the mayor's building, then back to the guy with the contract for paving the neighborhood streets from Armitage to Diversey, in a viable gyro of favor asked and granted.

Chicago: heavy, full, almost *sentient,* skies.

▲

The next I remember, Thick is arguing vigorously with a buffalo-shouldered fellow who owns a tow truck: and its hook has been slipped beneath the lip of our car as smoothly as if this were a how-to film on landing bass. *Hey buddy, MANAGEMENT ONLY,* this opponent keeps repeating, with the adamancy of a natural force or a backhoe, and first he points at the sign above our space that says exactly that, then points with relish at our junky (and clearly NON-managerial) car.

But FRIENDS of the manager, I hear Thick say through the muzziness, and there's dropping-of-names, and flashing-around-of-cash, and finally the little lotiony smiles of a purchased agreement.

—Politics.

The following morning I wake up with my father on my mind.

—Strange bedfellows.

ANCIENT EGYPT/
FANNIE GOLDBARTH

▲

Qebehseneuf

William Petty in the seventeenth century attained considerable notoriety
when he began to anatomize Anne Green, a murderess, and found that she
revived under his scalpel.

—Douglas Hay, Albion's Fatal Tree

I want this poem to be that black
she saw.
   The peccary
roadkill-death made general,
made an indication of peccaryness
—like an animal on a tavern sign—
that children are afraid to touch
in the lobby display of the Austin Nature Center . . .
she looked that far
beyond reclamatory powers. If
she did "dress flash," all razz and sass,
to cheat them of another scabby doxie in rags gone
weeping to do "the air jig" at the Hanging Tree,
if she stepped in the cart with a wedding gown on
and "flipped a fullmoon arse" at the crowd
from out of her cloud of bridewhite satin and taffeta,
and took the rope singing, took it on arteries
winged out wide in singing,
       she was an ashen satchel
of death on the table, her only other colors
a mustard-green and muddied plum in the shape
of a braid biting into her throat. You could feel
its hard and regular ridges . . .
      Now
a small boy's screaming. The guide asks why.
She bends to the haunch of the peccary,
where he's wild-eyed with horror, and asks.
He knows she knows he's seen

For chronology, see note on acknowledgments page.

a shock of excelsiorwork and taxidermist's carving
through a peeled patch, and *that* he can tell her.
But how can he say
near Chimney Hill is a giant revolving cowgirl
sign, for some motel, but broken, so
by night you can see her fluorescent
ribcage glowing.

▲

An Indian medical text of the 15th century
discusses closing intestinal wounds by lining
black Bengali ants along the rupture. Really.
They clamp it together. Their bodies are snapped off
and the jaws remain, as ample sutures
that dissolve by the time the wound heals. But—why
think of it? There she is, so
small. And when she sleeps she's even smaller.
My mother. The tubes running into her. That,
and the language they use! . . . "cut her open." "do a little
exploratory." Yes, and when the last ant vanished,
then the bowel could be coiled back into the abdomen and
sewn up. A way of thinking of her now
I can return from. So small. A sleeping pill
has vanquished her, a pill the size of a typed *o*. She
will float that dark all night and wake
to gulp a breath of living, once, then sink through ether
back to the dark. And the language they use! . . .
They'll "put her under." The boy at the peccary
fainted. And was roused by the rub of a warm cloth.
Now I'm going to think about her in her oncology sheets
by thinking of him. But—deeper,
as her darkness is deeper.

▲

It was something like this
that Anne Green said: "Me mummy wor anged
fer er filch uf a barrister's quidpouch off is person
wot she coaxed wi er winkin an doveycoos
into a stoyt of ineebriation in is coach
OR SO THOY SAY, an me dud wor anged
the bleedin peabroyn fer is poachin
uf a wormy-eaded brace o doocks off a jodge's estate
OR SO THOY SAY, an me sis wor anged an me own
true luf, th idjit sot, wor anged
wi me poolin is legs to asten th end uf is sooferin, AN
OY by Gawd an Satan an evury sober Christian witness
wor anged—AN CAME BACK! *(a pause—the children*
in the street are the only ones who will listen a third
or fourth or seventeenth time to her tale, but they
listen rapt, and her stagey pacing takes direct effect)
O it wor dark. O it wor blacker n noyt, o
blacker n ink on a printers thomb, an me darlins
oy felt black as Death meself alriddy
standing onder th oistin tree wi me own pine coffin
alongmeside loyk a woyt woyt shadow, everthin wor so black!
Loyk oy wor lookin into a scuttle o coaldust,
broyt, an soft, an in it me mum an dud an sis
an rumwit Arry isself who oy luffed so dear
was callin me COME ERE COME ERE COME ON IN
AN KISS US IN THIS ERE SWEET BLACK DUST when
uf a sudden it wor loyk a and ad snatched me op
an out an a voice sayin This
ere lattle coal lump still gots a bit o waitin an
burnin to do. *(wink)* An
whan oy opened me oyes
oy foun a Surjun bleenkin
ployin wi me bubbies in a pooblic ployce!"

▲

Mother, the gut is the longest of us.
It's 30 feet. It's our gravity, dragging.

Weren't you always ahead of us? Parting the traffic?
Testing the waves at the beach?

I once saw a gull there soar from its offal
so easily—air, parting air.

And mother, without it you'll simply be
the closest of us to flying.

▲

Tutankhamun's intestines
were folded in linen, then
set in a miniature mummiform coffin
"of beaten gold
inlaid with colored glass and carnelian."
On the inner lid, the goddess Selket is
traced in the gold with her wings spread, proclaiming,
in glyph script falling like rain about her,
Now I place my arms on that which is given to me:
Qebehseneuf, who is now within my protection.
—More traditionally,
the simple stone "canopic jar" was used.
On this, the lid was carved
as the hawk-headed god and spirit-of-the-intestines
Qebehseneuf, and there might not even be an inscription.
Even so, his guardian beak is sharp and,
always, the worker who fashioned him has placed the eyes
in focus on a plane that we can only say
extends itself into Eternity.

▲

Rotogravure. Lorgnette. Dagnabbit.
Some words truly die. But others . . .
Anne Green may have been like that: grabbed
last-minute out of her final blackflamed burning;
given second breath. She might be,
as these words are . . . quaint. "Maw, lookee!
Thir goes th Crazy Lady!" "Leave er be,
poor thing wot promynods oldin conversoytion
wi erself." *Alembic. Roustabout. Phlogiston.*
O'er. In a conversation on poetics,
Galway Kinnell has talked of the singular pleasure
of salvaging junkheap words, of tuning them
lubed and ahum in new vehicles. *Mizzling,*
he uses, *stillic, droozed, bast, damozel, biestings*
—words be-aura'd with the ancient power of having touched
the fossil possibility inside themselves,
considered it, then turned and taken
one last fullfleshed clarionhood on a living tongue.
She might be, as these words are . . . charged.
Phlebotomist. Escutcheon. Swain.
The Lazarus Lady who entered that unrefusable black of the pit
and refused it. "Maw. . . ." "Hush! Lissen wot she be sayin."
Oracle Lady. Shaman Lady.
Black of the beetle, black of an ancestor's eyesockets.
Halcyon.
>   *Trilby.*
>   *Cameleopard.*
Lady who came back o'er.
Mugwumpery.
>   *Ectoplasm.*
>   *Pooch.*
>   *Scoot.*

▲

Mother, the skin is the least of us.
The rest, the most, has never been touched by light.

And it will be all right. But first you need to pilgrimage
boustrophedon through your own gut-dark.

And it will hurt. (I couldn't lie.)
The form of it may say rape, say death.

It isn't enough you're on your knees.
We want you on your back.

▲

The grass the blanket the grass. . . .
Livia was four—remember? We
picnicked in Humboldt Park and a group
of older girls asked if Livia could "go to the water"
with them (meaning the swimming pool all afternoon)
and you said yes, sure (meaning the drinking fountain)
—remember? And three hours later there you were
in a cop car cruising all the leafy bylanes and screaming
you'd kill yourself if you didn't find her, the cop
saying lady now lady, then Livia stalking calmly
up to the cop announcing she'd learned to swim

                                              —which
over the years has taken on the lustrous-verdigris surface
of myth.
              These sheets; the nurses' chalky uniforms;
the patients' pale faces (all are calla lilies
centered on pillows). . . . White. Such white. Like living
in an aspirin. White, and day and night an artificial
regimen of visits, and everything, time included,
dissolving. . . . You young again. Livia four. Me
squeezing the bark off a tree to study its grubs and
sun is on my cheek in a wedge as heavy and gold and
overhot as a slice of doublecheese pizza from Vito's
where Daddy's going to meet us. Your husband,
alive. Of course, alive, how crazy, 1956, and how come
Livia's not back yet with the girls, and light and
chlorophyll all over throwing soft aquarium
shadows on your own soft skin. . . .
                                        Now 30
years later, what is it
except the words we remember it in? The words
are everything, Mother.
                          The words we save
are the words we save everything else in.
                                          Really
what do we fear in looking at each other tonight
if not that every word we've said
so urgently between us all our lives

87

will herd at the edge of the memory record, stare
a moment into cloudiness, then step off . . .

                                        love

being foreplay for loss.

▲

In a friend's friend's house, I've seen a vast
and gaudy collection of whiskey decanters;
a hula girl, a golfer, a kilted and bagpiped Scot,
a circus clown, an aeronaut, an alpine yodeler . . .
"And here," he said and winked, "we keep our spirits."

▲

And here's the baboon-head canopic jar (the lungs).
And here's the jackal-head canopic jar (the stomach).
And here, a jar for grace (a mountain ibex).
And here, a jar for the brain (a dragonfly convoluting the air).
Or here, the mind (a dragonfly shadow).

▲

Dark. A few pills
circling in your system for a clock.
How strange, in this city of windowledge pigeons and sparrows,
to be in the world of Qebehseneuf the hawk,
that spirit, your totem, night's lid.

▲

And this is what we cherish: words
with one foot over the precipice,
called back
                  to bodies again. In some
Medieval Hebrew manuscripts, the text
is done so finely, with such supple twists, as to be given
entirely over to forming the bodies of human beings,
beasts, and birds. . . .
                        A single "paragraph" might draw
the picture of two grass-appraising oxen, a parrot their
same size, fish, a huge central tree with a husband and wife
enjoying a supper under its reach, each leaf a word, each feather,
scale, flex of flesh. . . .
                        The whole of Creation, literally
from language, as it was "In the beginning . . . The Lord
said 'Let there be. . . .'"
                        Now what does He think
of a hospital, Mother? All of these bodies,
seen from His height, bent by the needs of their hundred
individual easings. What word
are we part of? *Tenderness. Torture.* A woman asleep,
and a man with his head in his hands like a flashlight
shining on her all night, afraid if it blinks off once. . . .
                                              At
least we're still in His dictionary. An early 14th-century Bible
from Germany speaks of a "great fish" and this text comprises
Jonah being heaved from the jaws of a whaleish thing.
How long he'd been lost in pain in that gut!
In darkness unimaginable! And here he is,
arms open in wonder, as if the creature is
comicbook-like speaking him
into the light of the page.

▲

It was something like this
that Anne Green said (in translation): "I touched it.
I was there, I wore Death's black chemise.
Death took me partying. I swigged black hootch.
(The tongue has 10,000 buds and not one burned.)
I danced. I danced the black shimmy.
I shot black craps. The dice are black
and their markings are equally black. (Nobody wins.)
I rode in Death's luxury Caddie: mobster-black,
with monster fins and a one-way meter. Oh
children, listen: I was in Death's library. There
is only one entry in Death's thesaurus, "black," and then
a thousand thousand synonyms. Death's own
bed is black, and Death's lubricants black, and Death's sex
is a black prosthetic penetrating blackness. Listen,
oh children of mine: when Death was sleeping I
went for a walk on Death's black estate.
I undid the black deadbolt and slipped out alone.
The sky was like black acetate. The black grass sighed.
And something—who knows what?—but something . . .
—or how or why? But this: I heard my name being called
far off, *Anne Greeeeen,* or someone, maybe one of you,
but someone, saying *Mother.* Simply: *Mother.* Fastened,
strapped black in a black seat bolted black to the deck / some
marlin yanked me out and over
the waters, it hurt, I must have blacked out, I flew, and when
I opened my eyes light stung inside me like a white whip of salt.

▲

da Vinci played a joke.
In Rome. The court of the Medicis.
Fancy schmancy. All the dinner guests
with ziggurats of painted snails and candied goose brains,
that kind of thing. What Leonardo did: he
inflated the entrails of a large ram with a bellows,
and from around a corner he launched those by-now
overballooning intestines floating
blimpwise into the room
                        —Why think of it now? Bengali ants. . . .
Why say it? Eviscera spiraled by hand
(like boat rope) into their proper Egyptian ceramic. . . .
And she's so delicate now, I think my touching her direct
could break her. So I need these gloves,
these images.
I need facts
returned from where she's a guest tonight
in the realm of the uttermost, returned but
in bearable form.
                Or you might
or I might break.

▲

This morning. And its whetstone dazzle.
Even through the shade of this immensely full-bouffant Chicago elm,
such light . . . its
edge could sharpen surgical blades.
They'll be shaving her now. . . . So bright. . . .
                                        Qebehseneuf,
hawk-god, guardian, weight it darker, a little, bring
the ageless rind of blackness I've seen smiling
in the mouth of your jar. A little. A hypo's worth.
A shot of inoculate
blackness up a vein, no more.
The band of black that blanks the skies each night and some nights
says, in the whisper-rush of roaches, in the oilblots under parked cars, it
refuses to yield, and
yet it yields. That blackness. Bring it. Be with me.
Take my affidavit. Listen: I pledge my pulse.
Attend her. Be gentle. They snug their handsize
ether-mask against the mouth and nose, and then it's endless
floatingfloating the anthracite-black backwash of the brain
until a person is revived; if. And Qebehseneuf,
see that she is. Reprieve her. Agitate for archangelic and
gubernatorial pardon. Black: Houdini's-top-hat-black: the flowers
disappear but the point is, pop back
later umpteenfold. Perform that magic. Saw and rebuild her. Pass that
inky fifth of blackberry brandy out, until she passes out,
and be there when she comes-to. Hawk-god, listen:
I'm just me. I try to write these poems, be middling decent
with a lady, not add overmuch malarkey to the thickening
slick of it filming this planet—for me it's enough
to enter another day. But you can enter rooms through walls,
you're a god, can enter through the protein of a body,
ride the hemoglobin, be there. Qebehseneuf:
be there. See the honest justice done. The first
incision now. . . . This meat doll, on their slab. . . . Be
in communion. Show your shape. Prescribe a draft of black
regurgitant. *Take two black every black.* Be her bannister.
Ready her, steady her, black a rhizome thrives in. That
rebounding black Anne Green saw, dozed in, rose from

cockadoodling with her noosed voice; and the black some words
return from, saved by maybe just a few
such uses as this: *Cahoots. Peruke. Hotdiggity.*
Potentate. Flummoxed. Tootsies. Imbroglio. Cuirass. Suzerainty.
I'm just me in the sun,
just me in the threshing of dust and light,
the deckled depositions of high tide over the shale,
the way the cosmos beats us like a good pimp
so no bruises show and then we shake back out to the street
and work for it, here in the sweetness
at the bullseye of pleasureful sex, and with whatever
rabbinical wisdom in our blood is mumbling
holiness and prohibitions, me in the morning,
me a halfass pinball-play in the maze of Chicago traffic,
walking, talking to an ancient Egyptian
idea of things, and a word even older,
as if she might hearken
and come to me as she always did when I needed her,
                    me in the root of it,
                    out in the weather.
                         Please.

Mother.

▲

The kids are filing out of the Austin Nature Center.
"Whass that?"—one points.

The building's front is total glass. And the woman says,
"Small birds might crash here and die.

So these are the shapes of hawks
we put up cut from black paper.

A bird gets close enough, it spots the black hawks,
and it wheels right back where it came from."

Repairwork

The *whang!* of their anger back-and-forth
like a *jai alai* ball. . . . The souring pericardium. . . .
Friends halfway across the country are having their first
bad marital talons-out fight. What timing: I'm
here with a non-refundable ticket to visit them, waiting
for the PA's silver voice to call my flight. Last night
they phoned me (individually) and each opined half-heartedly
I "might help." Yeah, well I'm about one-thirtysecond-heartedly
convinced; and still, we *want* to believe in the efficacy
of magic healing: Jesus' human hands
inhumanly running over a leper's skin, as if
reversing the nap of a carpet; Reverend Hoodoo's
Jinx Removing Lucky Money Oil. Yes, and somewhere
in a thatch-and-quonset village in the Philippines,
they're lining up to see the "psychic surgeon,"
who will *flash* his bare hand into their bare bellies,
plucking out
the bloody gob of their malaise
without a pucker, not a paper cut,
in evidence the next day. Or
the story of the tailor
set to fashion the Emperor's coronation suit
on pain of death—who in his weary labors
sleeps before he's finished, but the mice
who he's befriended with his nightly rinds
observe this, and complete the ornate flaps and frogging
for him, lifting needles in their paws like swords,
and turning the buttons as if they were
great wheels in a cockpit. Maybe I should have seen
a wonder that extreme, the day
they gurneyed my mother into the ward, her gut
redone: they'd slit it first, like any other casing,
and when they were finished with that, they made of her
a piece of her clumsy seventh-grade sewing
from Home Economics so many years back.

It didn't have the exotic panache
and lightning-striking deftness of that Philippines repairwork;
but it held. It left its telltale signs
and exacted its telltale wage from her,
from us, it was a lesson in the languages of pain
and in the pain beyond all language,
but it held—its stitches held.
I land. Nobody's here to meet me
(like, should *he* come? *she* come?—well then,
neither comes). Some week it's going to be.
I nod at a taxi. I think of everyone
filling a taking-off plane—a hundred guts.
A hundred question marks.
It loses itself up there, a needle
into endless sky-blue cloth.

The Route

*For several moments he was lost in thought and then he straightened up
and looked at me, and his eyes burned with demoniac fire. "I can be master
of a world," he said; "perhaps I can even be master of the universe."*
—Edgar Rice Burroughs, *Swords of Mars*

Five a.m., and headlight-eating clots of fog
the size of cars approach my car the whole way
from Columbia, Missouri, to Saint Louis.
In Chicago, my mother is being carried by cancer
over the threshold of a next world,
and she fights it, but she goes
an inch a day, and with such pain
as only miles could measure, only an odometer
of suffering. By noon or maybe one I should arrive.
By seven a.m., the fog is rising from the trees,
is like the huge ghost of a raptor
trying still to lift its prey. "Igor,
fetch me a nice fresh brain" is what you'd think
to hear in this grim landscape—and, as if on cue,
the radio seizes on a wretched drama of medical genius
foully mushroomed into megalomania: "I hope
to rule the world with an army of such as these!"
then a trail of nyeh-heh-hehs. I punch it off. This
simpy play at horror pales next to the real
familial thing. By eleven, I'm into
the sprawl of outskirts smokestacks
—sweating, with the car a.c. on *freeze.* My mother
dwindling in her danglework of tubes.
My mother monitored at the tip of a needle.
If only the morphine does its job. If only
there's one more good day left. Now
that would be hope, that would be goddam hope
and mad science enough for me.

Prepositions

We are going _____ *the moving picture theater. (direction)*
Tim will pick us up _____ *eight o'clock. (time)*
Rifke sits curled on my mother's plastic-covered fuchsia couch
and looks up from her primer. She tells me "In Moscow—"
then she points to herself "me—Rifke—big, big—" hands
try sculpting a building from air, as if from snow "big
arshitaker." "Architect?" "Da, da, archiTEK!
Chicago? Houses—POOY! In Moscow—BYOO-tee,
the houses!" Now she lives in this unbeautiful house
for 75 American bucks per day, and tends to my mother,
whose cancer is spread from her lung to a traitorous
system of bones that lead to the small of the back. No
language is adequate to *her* future; soon she'll only speak
to the rest of us as memory. Rifke, meanwhile,

uses every filch of minutes between a pill and a bath,
a meal and a pill, a pill and a tearing up of the bowels,
to practice. "Ahlboort—this—what?" Ahlboort,
big—big—poet, doesn't know. *The house is* _____
the corner. (location) On? at? near? around? by? Rifke
polishing each sentence in her mouth. My mother
speaking in the nuances of moan. This week I'm visiting,
its pablums and the blotchy shout of skin
around where the chemo needle sidles in . . .   so many new
unbearable things to be borne. It's even sadder
in the basement, where my father's pea-green office surplus
work desk carries the neatly-nibbed accounts-&-debits lists
of 1970 on its back like a time capsule burro—sadder,
but easier too, since death and the whisk of long years

following death have lightened the room of physical suffering,
have reduced that to a level of mementos: all
of his carbon paper and springs from clicker ballpoint pens
and the sponge for moistening labels, five-and-dime supplies
that even in 1970 had been long since superseded
by a fast-track, ever-electromutational planet. Rifke
too: her schoolbook exercises creakily invite her *Let us*
attend the newsreel "movie" _____ *the gang. (together),* and
Perhaps we can stay _____ *the "short." (intention),* words
that fluttered out the open window of a Hudson or DeSoto
decades back, and were never returned for. Now
the alternations of sun and snows have worked them into
ghost words; though for a while they were here, and
filled the blankness that we come from and we go to.

A Still Life, Symbolic of Lines

It's aesthetically lovely, but pangs the mind
—the way in Aubrey's *Lives* the whole of sixty, seventy years
is fit in one well-loaded line. Of Sir Jonas Moore:
Sciatica: he cured it by boyling his Buttock. And so
those anguished nights, the days of frenzied panacea-shopping,
go by in eight words. Or of Mary Rich, Countess of Warwick:
Shee needed neither borrowed Shades, nor reflexive Lights,
to set her off, being personally great in all naturall Endowments,
click. One day there won't even be Aubrey around, just
dust in skirling threads through the silicon chips, and then
even these relict lines will be gone, will be mulch,
will be dander hoarded by ants. I've tried to do it today

with my father: one line. But I can't choose. *Since his work day*
was 12 hours, it compressed his love for his family,
in the remaining hours, past their understanding. That's
a real possibility: for truth, if not for eloquence. (Or
more than 12: up all night, in that basement "study"
—one desk, over the drain hole—where the nickels
for our bargain-table shoes and our sweaters from "seconds" stores
were fossicked out of his leather-look plastic ledger books.)
He'd put on his salesman's smile the way somebody else might
pin on a badge of great office—that's also, I think,
a contender. But you'd have to have known my father
to appreciate these, while Aubrey's prose makes strangers

clear. Isaac Barrow: *He was a strong man, but*
pale as the Candle he studyed by. Or: *In love with Geometry, . . .*
Thomas Hobbes *. . . was wont to draw lines on his thigh*
and on the sheets, abed. I'm reading Aubrey back at the house
my seventy-six-year-old mother still lives in—reading him,
one of the few books that I've brought for the week I'm helping her
post-surgery heal, dampened gauzey strip by gauzey strip.
He's good on suffering: *To Cure the Tooth-Ach, Take a new Nail,*
and make the Gum bleed with it, and then drive it into an Oak.
This did cure Sir William Neal's Son, when he was Mad with the Pain.
But really: it's time to close that book, it's time
to face each stitch in my mother, and start to learn the lesson

of pain: how something inside us not even the size
of a fish egg clouds the ceiling of this crackerbox house
with thick gray wafts of lamentation, and funnels
into the sour, cul-de-sac shadow in the toe of a shoe.
It's time to change the pads again, and freshen the salves.
It's time to retrace—reravel—the trails of thingness in this place
where I was raised, and where his presence is a lingering,
ghost-swirled weather. Things: the Bible
in its silver filigree cover; the yuk-yuk naughty
heads-or-tails coin still "hidden" under his handkerchiefs;
the dimestore pie safe (one-ply tin) with dings by now
as acute as the lunar surface. . . . Remember *Plotto?*

—"a thick, expensive book containing brief, algebraic
descriptions of every possible story construction
known to mankind." In the '30s and '40s, writers for the pulps
resorted regularly to its riches. All the plotlines
extended as niftily as if a surveyor had done them;
what you simply had to do was add persuasive *objets,*
a treasure map, an obsidian idol, a smoking purse-size gun,
at the lines' conjunctions. And here, in the house
of my own small history?—his rubberbanded note cards
with the names of clients A to Z, his *kiddush* cup
for the ritual wine, his cheap police-band radio . . .
persuasive *objets.* And surely if I were sensitive enough

to these, the narrative of who he was, and who my mother is,
would boldly write itself across the air, with a clarity
and a finality beyond question. Of course it doesn't work
that way. I rummage and muddle. Tonight I sit
at his desk in the basement. The desk is a dark and dull pea-green
(the office surplus color of 1955), and so is the 40 watts down here,
and the splattered blotter—murkily, khakily dingy.
Nearly shouting out from all this is the gummyish pink
of his old friends and saviors—the lozenge kind
for pencil, and the flat disc kind for ink, things phasing
right now out of cultural use themselves. A still life, symbolic
of lines; of lines and their erasure.

The description of Plotto *is from Lee Server's* Danger Is My Business.
*John Aubrey: "How these curiosities would be quite forgott, did not such idle fellowes as I am
putt them downe."*

Deer

The Captain [Chicago Tribune mogul Joseph Patterson] had many burdens, and one of them was his pampered socialite daughter, Alicia, who in 1942 made up her mind she was darn well going to write a new comic strip for her old man's syndicate. Few strips were released amid noisier fanfare and greater expectation. Few proved to be such monumental disasters so fast.

Deer was an ancient Egyptian princess who, when professors cracked open her sarcophagus, reawoke in 1940's New York City and proceeded to embark on a thriller-diller of an adventure involving gangsters, Middle Eastern brigands and a lost treasure. She had a boyfriend named Bruce and a pet falcon that had accompanied her on the immortal journey from the grave.

. . . Time magazine ridiculed it as the worst comic strip in history. Mortified, the mighty Tribune-News organization pulled the plug on "Deer" —in mid-story—after just nine months.

—from Jay Meader's chronicle of the
Tribune-News comic strips,
A Unique American Art: 100 Years of the Funnies

Gumshoes, shamuses, private-eyes, -dicks, ops, are terms
in the hardboiled air of 1942. Their hellspawn counterparts
are mobsters, gangsters, Machiavellian Mr. Bigs or simple
gunsels: thugs and goons and their corseted cohorts, molls.
Not that the roles themselves are very different, ever: these
eternal *noir* and boudoir personalities are who a human being *is*,
if structured *in extremis*. In the Thebes of ancient Egypt, too,
as the wheel of flies and the wheel of Ra's resplendent solar travel
roll incessantly: "then did the pilferers descend, with clubs
and many a savage cry; and the guards at the fishery gates
in the name of Pharaoh did rout them." Though the ivy tower
ethereum-minds at State U may exquisitely fuss at the differences
defining Culture A from Culture Z, the wiseguy, streetsmart,
roll-with-the-pummeling-punches, opportunity-savvy,
Real-Life-As-We-Know-It Dwellers amongst us ease through any
interworld transition with nary a doubtful pause
of their one-two piston fists, with nary a flicker of their wary
mascara'd eyes. "She slipped him knockout drops in his hootch
—you know, a mickey finn" becomes, *sans* even the iffiest glitch,
". . . and did stir in his portion of wine the juice of the poppy."
A .45 is a "rod," a "gat," a "chattering roscoe,"
and brass knuckles are "bucket dusters," and a blackjack is a "sap," some bubba
sucking a stogie wants to lam it pronto with the boodle
—and this is eminently translatable back-and-forth between
the juke dives sullenly clustered along the Chicago River and those
that hug the Nile. So when Deathless Deer and dreamboat
boyfriend Bruce are licketysplitting through the alleys
with a splinter cult of (evil) Egyptian priests hot on their tail,
the story is instantly and achronally recognizable. "Darling,
here!"—and they duck into the vent-shaft of the hospital

▲

where my mother is a territory further claimed each morning
by the cancer. You could trace her name and her dates
in the thickening residue it's leaving
on the lining of her lungs. "You see how the needle fits? Come look,"
she shows me her I.V. hookup, "Albert, I know *you,* all right: you'll put it
in a poem." Even now—her final, frail days—she can't stop
helping me. It's 1995, she's 78, she's dying daily by the handful, and
she's helping *me:* the story of her unassuming and others-enabling,
meritorious life. My mother this pale paste in a garnish
of medical wire. Because we know now that this poem
is an example of Existence as a working synchronasium
—an endlessness of analog-points freefloating in Time, that
sometimes touch—I sit at her bedside direly keening
inside myself a version of an earlier people's litany:

When the shirts wore out, she still saved the buttons
Now she's a quiet moan; the orderlies sometimes hearken, sometimes not
Her husband came, her nipples stiffened into umber thimbles
Now the cigarettes of sixty years are refuse dumps inside her
She saved the buttons, the thread, the crusts of the bread
Now they study her chart, they confer, they say no
When she posed on the lion statue, she was 23 and electric
Now she speaks—it's like a voice from a pool of tallow
She'd have saved the hair from her shaved legs if she could, and found a use
Now they bathe her: hosing down an animal in its zoo cage
Every night she rinsed the black gunk from the dog's eyes, gently, patiently
Now she says: "Why won't God take me? Aren't I good enough?"
She saved: it became my college, she saved: my sister's college
She threw away my comic books, she played her nickel poker games
She carried the burning caraway seed of a dream inside her, like anyone
Now nothing will save her: nothing will save her

▲

—meanwhile, *here!* "and they duck into the vent-shaft of the hospital."
Deer of course is amply familiar with that fat, deep-teal noun
of a thing, a duck: she's gorged its dribbling meat, she's
watched them court and squabble in the marshes; having
seen them feed—a *plink!* beneath the surface—this forthrightly simple
Anglolingo verb is no great mystery; the vent-shaft, no great fright
to someone risen from a mummy case. The truth is, at this
chronospatial fold in the continuum, most of everything
has easy correspondence; the Chicago news is full of powermongers
not so different from these renegade, black-magic-practitioner priests
who have stolen ("heisted," *we'd* say, or "lightfingered") a slender phial
of the Elixir of Immortality from its proper, immemorial place
in the Temple of Ra. Deer's stolen it back—but barely; and
this zealous pursuit of Evil hotfooting it after Beauty and Good
is, as we see in the primary colors of the Sunday comics, broken
through the linkstitch of Sequential Time itself. And so
they're here now, in this hallway, in this poem, milieuxed
cartoonily in the kind of drama most of us only know
as a small and day-to-day erosion of the heart. Deer says,
"Our peril is grave. The Vulture Priest himself has chosen
to follow me into your realm." Bruce says, "So *that's* his moniker,
is it? Well, cupcake—he's sporting a mug to match."
The frantic minutes that they spend in stealth eluding this pursuit
go by for us as seven-times-a-week installments of a story
—in the Laundry Room, the Kitchen, and amid fantastic shadows
cast by the Gothic contraptions of Rehab and Hydrotherapy.
"Bruce, they are nearly upon us!" "We'll have to stash
our little item for now, and make our sweet selves scarce."
So: hastily picking through a locker labeled *Supplies,*
"Bruce darling, quickly! Pour it in this!"—"this"

▲

being my mother's next morphine bag. So, in this poem,
the Elixir of Immortality enters her bloodstream. Not that this
has anything viable to do with her suffering *off* of the page
—she bloats in parts and withers in others, and sometimes
seems to whimper at even the weight of the cotton sheet.
But there's that other world—of concepts, and of gods
whose job is representing concepts. Some days, one
corrupted node in my mother the size of an infant's thumbnail
logs in pain enough to vastly outbalance cosmology,
theology, ethics, and all of the gassier -isms. And yet, and ever . . .
there's that other world, of formulae, and liturgical chants . . .

    I saw Anubis walking the halls—Dr. Anubis, they called him here
He wrote his prescriptions: Death, take people as needed
    Anubis walking the halls—the Devourer
His stethoscope drank up every heartbeat it listened to
    I saw Horus, the Hawk, he was scrubbing up
The silhouette of his head on the wall: a medieval surgical scraper
    I saw Nut, whose arching body is the sky
And as the stars came out, the shrieks of the world grew louder
    Thoth the Scribe and rounded Hapy and stingtailed Sekhmet
The gods on break, the gods at cards in the cafeteria
    I don't want to know the stakes for that game
I don't want to know who won, who lost
    I saw Osiris, the Giver of Life, the Breather of Resurrected Life
Some rooms, he stopped at; only some
    Or maybe I didn't see them, but they were there
Like gin in the watermelon: invisible spirits, invisible spirits
    For all of the good the oncologist and his chemo did my mother
Let Anubis walk the halls, let Osiris walk the halls
    Let their always-was and never-ending fight be the explanation

▲

—meanwhile, the life of the body goes on.
Despite all of my poetry hokeypokey-and-parsley, the life
of the body—the cellular fundament, the clock—goes on
until its final electrolytic tick of time.
Decay goes on. The grain by grain dissolving
continues as formidably as the bud by bud *in utero* accreting-together
did. When my sister visits she asks if my mother believes
she'll be "in heaven—with Daddy." The slyly
fearful/wishful noncommital answer: "I *hope* so." This,
in a voice like a sliver of soap disappearing in being used.
The following day my sister holds her hand
for hours, while whatever "self" is left of herself, inside of herself,
flutters like a moth in search of an exit,
wearily beats at the cancerous lumpgrown underside of the skin.
There is no magic elixir for this, no out-of-the-empyrean
deific intervention—no, there's only the pissy arguing now
with a clod of a doctor over what he airily calls "pain management"
(too little too slow), and the true heart-sundering moments
when her eyes clear and that 23-year-old life-fixated woman
on the lion statue stares at me from out of this sunken-in form.
That's it. That's everything. That's the whole world today.
And as for Deathless Deer and her beau and their villainous foes . . .
I don't know, and I can't care; but I think I've done
what I wanted to do: they're out of the hospital,
out of the limbo of cancellation in 1942, I see them
turn a corner out of sight ("Scramola this way, kiddo,"
says Bruce) and they're bringing their rollicking caper anew
to the dangerous streets of America. I've given her a second chance.
(It's easy: she's not "really" "alive.") Now I turn back
to my mother's bed on July 23rd 1995.

Albert Goldbarth is Distinguished Professor of Humanities in the English department at Wichita State University. He is the author of many volumes of poetry, including *The Gods, Popular Culture,* and *Marriage, and Other Science Fiction.* He is the recipient of the National Book Critics Circle Award, the Chad Walsh Memorial Award, and the Ohio State University Press/*The Journal* Award in Poetry.